SACRAMENTO PUBLIC LIBRARY

3 3029 04772 1337

MARTIN LUTHER KING, JR
LIBRARY
7340 - 24TH STREET BYPASS
SACRAMENTO, CA 95822

D0464844

MAR 2 5 2003

COLOR STORIES

STORIES

BEHIND THE SCENES OF AMERICA'S

BILLION-DOLLAR BEAUTY INDUSTRY

MARY LISA GAVENAS

SIMON & SCHUSTER

NEW YORK   LONDON   TORONTO   SYDNEY   SINGAPORE

SIMON & SCHUSTER
Rockefeller Center
1230 Avenue of the Americas
New York, NY 10020

Copyright © 2002 by Mary Lisa Gavenas
All rights reserved,
including the right of reproduction
in whole or in part in any form.

SIMON & SCHUSTER and colophon are registered trademarks
of Simon & Schuster, Inc.

For information regarding special discounts for bulk purchases,
please contact Simon & Schuster Special Sales
at 1-800-456-6798 or business@simonandschuster.com

Manufactured in the United States of America

1   3   5   7   9   10   8   6   4   2

Library of Congress Cataloging-in-Publication Data
Gavenas, Mary Lisa.
Color stories: behind the scenes of America's billion-dollar
beauty industry / Mary Lisa Gavenas.
        p. cm.
1. Cosmetics industry—United States. 2. Beauty culture—United States. I. Title.
HD9970.5.C673 U5438   2002
338.4'764672'0973—dc21   2002026822
ISBN 0-684-86515-7

CONTENTS

COLOR
STORIES

Preseason

WHAT'S IN STORE

HERE IN BELLEVUE, eight miles into Seattle's suburbs, the weather is chilly, drizzly, and gray. At the town's immense indoor mall, the big post-holiday clearances are over. Spring sales haven't started yet. Listless salespeople stand around, staring down almost empty aisles.

Except in beauty. Blue skies shine out of every picture in the cosmetics department. Hot, happy colors cover the counters. Every counter has a story and every story speaks of sunny days ahead. Customers are all over the place. And salespeople, "beauty advisors," are run off their feet: squirting perfume, doing makeovers, ringing up sale after sale.

Any destination, any route—into the mall, out to the parking garage, up the escalator—takes you right through cosmetics. Straight into a world where there's always something you can afford. Where one size fits all. Where nobody is stingy with samples and nobody nags if you hang around.

Here are thousands of things you can wear. Plus gimmicks like "Plastic Shine" to make your mouth glossy as a magazine cover. One counter's got compacts decorated with the angel of your birthday month—who knew there was such a thing? Then there's all that other stuff they come up with, like chakra nail polish and bubble bath that smells like cinnamon buns. A woman would have to go almost every day to keep track.

Some do. "Anything new?" asks a woman who was here the day before yesterday. The beauty advisors greet her by name and tell her. "This is new!" a connoisseur announces approvingly as she twirls a sparkly wand that wasn't around last week. Others cruise the counters, on their way to somewhere else, wondering "What's new?," keeping tabs on gift-with-purchase deals, looking over the latest.

At Lancôme, three women watch the spring makeup video without understanding a word of its French. At Origins, a thirteen-year-old fidgets through her first makeover as a beauty advisor got up in a gardening apron plants Rhubarb on her lips, brushes Fringe Benefits on her lashes, and dusts Sunny Disposition across her cheeks. At Clinique, a beauty advisor with a Germanic accent, dressed in what looks like a lab coat, lectures on lipsticks with volatile silicones.

Later today, the store's having another one of its special events. A Bobbi Brown makeup artist, someone who works on big-name models on big-time runways, will be doing makeovers. For free. You don't have to buy a thing. And before that starts, a slew of video monitors will be showing Bobbi backstage at the shows.

Come to the beauty department. Hear what's new. Get out of the house for a while. Dab and sample and swipe the colors. Pour your heart out to someone who will pat soothing creams on your forehead and caress your cheek with pretty powders. Check out the videos. Find out why what's coming will be better than what's past. Change your life. Change your mood.

Even on the slowest day, there's something good going on in beauty.

They make it so easy. Beauty is at the entrance and exit of the store, where you find yourself all the time. They get you coming and going. No reservations needed. No appointment necessary. No obligation to buy.

Today, the store has only been open a few minutes when the first one comes to the counter.

"I need a new lipstick."

On her way to the mall this morning, she pulled her lipstick out of her purse and put it on in the rearview mirror, just like always. She swiped her same pink across the top half of her mouth, then the bottom. She rolled her lips together to get the color nice and even. Just like she does a half dozen times a day. Only this time, when she pushed the mirror back into place and backed out of the driveway, she suddenly felt blah, bored, tired of the same old routine.

So now, before she runs the rest of the day's errands, she finds herself standing at the Estée Lauder counter in Nordstrom. A nice woman is nodding sympathetically and saying, "I know exactly how you feel."

The nice woman leads her over to one of those seasonal collections that the beauty industry calls "color stories." The counter display has a catchy slogan, eye makeup and lipsticks with cute names, and a cardboard picture of the coming season that looks just about perfect. Beauty stories are always optimistic.

This one urges her to "Go Tropical." On the sign, a sultry spokesmodel smiles with the nonchalance of a woman who has never carpooled, shopped at a mall, or parked a minivan. Braless. Blithe. Bikini bottom showing her flat stomach and skinny thighs.

Below the picture of the model in her tropical paradise are about a half dozen pretty pink lipsticks, cute little pairs of eye shadows, two-ended pencils with a different color on each end, and a tube of—my God, is that really turquoise?—mascara. The woman picks up the mascara. She's never seen anything like it.

"I know," says the beauty advisor, flashing her conspiratorial, you-gotta-love-this-stuff grin. "Isn't it fun?"

While the beauty advisor runs through her spiel about "instant gratification" and "doing something for yourself," the woman slowly strokes a pencil across the back of her hand. She pokes at the eye shadows. She smudges and speculates. She picks up lipsticks and swipes them on her hand. She squints and stares at the swipes. Well, a new lipstick isn't going to break the bank.

She's buying it: the picture of the model in her bikini bottom, playtime at the counter, everything the beauty advisor is telling her about warm-weather trends. After contentedly covering her hand with pink and purple smears, she settles on Pareo, a pink lipstick that looks pretty much like the one she put on in the car this morning. It's not the same, though. It's what she didn't have before. It's what's in that picture of spring.

The beauty advisor rings up the sale and tosses in a sample of the latest skin lotion. The woman, now beaming, doesn't bother to put on her new Pareo. She's already running late. She grabs her little package and hurries into the main mall. She got what she came for.

Spring looks different. Warm and relaxed. Lush and a little luxurious.

She owns a piece of it already.

"This is a *great* story," declares Debbie Danekas, as she watches her first customer of the day hurry happily away.

Debbie loves a good color story. It gets women to her counter. When women wander up Debbie can start talking about the color story. "I try to ask as many questions as I can. What she wears, what is she looking for . . . if she has an idea, then we can help her achieve that."

Some women have very specific reasons for being in the beauty department, like getting ready for a new job or accessorizing an outfit or treating themselves. Some come for beauty therapy. "If I can make someone look good and they have problems," Debbie explains earnestly, "I can help take that away." If the transformation in her customers is sometimes more emotional than physical, that's okay too: "If you feel good, you feel good. And if you look good, you feel good."

Debbie, who's in her mid-forties, used to work in the resort industry, and her style of salesmanship falls somewhere between the compassion of a good priest and the competence of a good concierge. Her belief in her beloved beauty products is absolute. Thirteen Estée Lauder color cosmetics went on her own face this morning. A number, she is quick to remind you, that by no means reflects her entire routine since she also has to do body care and hair and fragrance. "And I do skin care before that."

Debbie doesn't have time to expound further, because another customer is steaming toward the counter. The last one was only wearing lipstick. This one is in full war paint. Purple lids. Fuchsia lips. Foundation. Mascara. Pencils. The works. This one doesn't have to be led to "Go Tropical." She makes a beeline for it.

"How are you today?" Debbie asks brightly.

Tapping the testers with an inch-long acrylic nail, this one gets straight to the point: "Pink. I'm in the mood for pink."

No matter what else is going on in the world, women head for the beauty department as if there's something there they can't find anywhere else. Whatever happens—good or bad—they keep coming. Celebrate or console, lipstick's always available. Lipstick always fits. It's always onward and upward in beauty.

By noon, they're overrunning the place. With the special event in full swing, the beauty department has become the epicenter of activity for the entire thirty-four-acre mall. Babies squall. Registers stutter out receipts. Sound ricochets off shiny-surfaced counters and floors while dozens of women try to make themselves heard.

"I can't lose ten pounds by tomorrow, so this will have to be it . . ."

"I wanna look like her . . ."

"I need a change . . ."

"I need eyes . . ."

"Transform me!"

Earlier this week, a newspaper ad invited customers to book a free makeover and get personal recommendations from a Bobbi Brown National Makeup Artist. During the next six hours, seventy-three of those respondents have to get their new faces. Wave after wave of walk-ins want new faces too.

Spillover stations are being improvised while names are taken. Just up the escalator from all this, Nordstrom's pianist scores the scene with one zingy show tune after another. Right now, he's up there in his tuxedo pounding out "My Funny Valentine."

Directly opposite the main makeover tables, a video monitor plays an endless loop of Bobbi Brown, the forty-something soccer mom from New Jersey whose own fascination with makeup made her a millionaire. Everyone here knows Bobbi's story.

As each customer arrives, she's checked in at a central counter and escorted to a station. Thus Sara, who's here because she's about to start a new job, is paired with the makeup artist who'll be working on her. Once the introduction is made, both switch to beauty-speak.

"I'm a true combination."

"Oily through the T-zone?"

"But because of my age, it needs hydrating . . ." and Sara makes a gesture of despair in the direction of her eyelids.

The two get down to work. As the makeup artist pats Eye Cream on Sara's lids, she says "Bobbi went to a woman dermatologist to develop this. Most are made by men and they just *can't* relate! They do not know!" Sad but true. Men just don't get it.

In view of about a hundred passersby, the makeup artist paints brown and yellow stripes down the side of Sara's face. While they wait to see which foundation will blend in best, Sara asks about makeup trends for next season.

"We're not really about that," the makeup artist says a little self-righteously. "Bobbi's philosophy is to make a woman look like herself—only pretty."

Fifteen or twenty minutes go by like this. Finally— after cleanser, eye makeup remover, moisturizer, eye cream, concealer, foundation, and a little powder— Sara is ready for some real makeup. The visiting specialist is called over to inspect her.

Clipboard against one hip, legs planted against all the women jostling for a good view of makeovers or monitors, the makeup artist who's worked on runway models is about to work her magic on Sara here at the mall. In not much more than a minute, she's ticked off seventeen products on a take-home application chart, giving Sara stories slugged "daytime," "career," and "evening." Before sweeping on to the next customer, she leans in to confide: "If you're ever feeling low and you need a lift? Bronzer! It makes you feel alive."

The pianist, who couldn't have heard her, chooses this moment to play "The sun'll come out tomorrow" music from *Annie*.

Seven more products and twenty more minutes of ministrations later, Sara's quick-and-easy career story is complete. Now it's time to clinch the sale.

"Do you wanna get the eye cream we talked about?"

The answer is no.

No hard feelings, the makeup artist knows Sara will be back to buy eventually. She hands Sara a mirror, along with the best compliment she can think of: "Your skin is so pretty! It doesn't look like you're wearing any makeup at all!"

Sara beams, eager to try out her new face, her new story.

All around her, women sit at makeup stations with rabbity, unmadeup eyes and bare faces, eager to get their own.

Beauty aspires to be all things to all women and comes close to succeeding. By best estimates, beauty in America is a $29 billion business. Beauty departments are top earners for any store. Beauty licenses subsidize French couture and buoy the bottom lines of the American fashion houses lucky enough to land them. Beauty contracts carry the biggest paydays, offer the most publicity, and are therefore the most coveted prizes in the modeling industry. Beauty trends have replaced hemlines as the hot news from runways. Beauty advertising is a mainstay of women's magazines. Beauty editorial always rates among the most-read pages in those same magazines.

Beauty history abounds with role models. Madam C. J. Walker, Elizabeth Arden, Helena Rubinstein, Harriet Hubbard Ayer, Bobbi Brown. Immigrants, African American women, women who never finished high school, divorced single moms, happily married soccer moms. Long before most women went into business, the beauty industry was creating female millionaires. Long after women MBAs began butting their heads on glass ceilings, the beauty industry glorified female go-getters.

Beauty profits are steady. Perfumes and makeup alone—categories that have no crossover with hygiene and no pretense of being necessities—account for at least $12 billion annually. Just the kind of makeup being sold here in the mall, which the industry refers to as its "prestige" segment, runs at least $2 billion a year.

Best of all, it's a business that never sees a downturn or suffers a serious setback. Not during wars. Not during depressions. America's fascination with beauty seems never ending, its demand for beauty products insatiable. The beauty industry has mastered not only how to give its customers what but how to keep them happily clamoring for more. This year, beauty industry profits will go up. Next year, they'll go up again. They always do.

A story. That's what women get when they come to the beauty counter. A parable that takes strange, scary styles and explains them as something any woman can own and wear. A diversion, an amusement, a distraction from woes and worries. A fantasy, a fable, a romance with a role for them to play.

For all its billions in profits, for all the sophisticated distribution deals and international wheeling and dealing, beauty remains a business of storytelling, an industry where market forecasts and number crunching inevitably yield to adjectives and atmosphere. The most successful companies are the ones that spin the fantasies that the most women want to hear. At the highest corporate level, decisions are based on storyboards pasted together of old magazine pictures. And anyone with a good enough story can still make it big in the beauty business.

Each spring and each fall, in a time cycle loosely tied to fashion, the beauty industry invents fresh stories to keep women coming to its counters. Each season the same rituals are repeated: Products are dreamed up, sent to the factory, packaged, advertised, and then shown to the press.

Behind that seemingly straightforward progression are dozens more characters and subplots. Each aspect of the business comes with its own quirky history. And each begets still more subplots and suspense. Which launch will bomb? Which runway looks will wind up winning the most magazine pages? How will women want to see themselves? What will be the story of the season?

Toward dinnertime, two soccer moms rush in from the parking garage, hellbent on some errand or other. They're making for the mall entrance, until they spot "Go Tropical" on the beauty counter.

Whatever that errand was, it will have to wait. Sticking their fingers in the little pans of powders, smudging colors on the backs of their hands, swiping lipsticks and pencils, they say, "Do you believe this?" and "What will they think up next?" Noticing the tube of turquoise mascara, they wave its little wand and giggle. Maybe they're trying to imagine themselves ambling around a sunshine-soaked tropical paradise where houseboys run their errands. Maybe they're trying to imagine themselves ambling around Bellevue with turquoise lashes.

"Isn't it fun?" says Debbie, who saw them coming. The two of them listen to her talk about sexy looks and hot colors and the summer ahead. It's a good story. They want to hear more.

So Debbie elaborates. She talks about next season's fashion with as much certainty as if she'd strolled the catwalks of New York and Paris herself. She tells them everyone will be in capri pants come summer. The two women in anoraks and jeans smile.

Debbie interrupts herself every once in a while to demonstrate a different product. "It's instant gratification," Debbie tells them, sounding very down-to-earth, very just-between-us. "Buying this makes you feel good. You can't just always sit down and buy clothes . . ." To complete that thought she gestures toward the story on the counter, as the two soccer moms nod in vigorous agreement.

The way she tells it, spring sounds absolutely wonderful. The longer they listen, the happier the two women look. Better days ahead. They want to hear about the next season, the next story.

Back in New York, the beauty industry is busy getting it ready for them.

November

PRODUCT DEVELOPMENT:
ONCE UPON A TIME . . .

SO MANY PEOPLE have been wearing makeup for so long that it's hard to imagine how anybody could come up with anything new. At this late date, just about everything has been done. Every possible permutation. Every conceivable refinement of color and its application to the human face.

This afternoon, it's Dominique Szabo's job to find another one. "The next one! The next one! Always the newest! The women love what is new. What will arrive at the counter? What is the surprise of the season?" she says excitedly, as she sits in her otherwise-serene office at Estée Lauder, floating thirty-nine floors above midtown Manhattan.

Right now, the rest of the world is gearing up for Thanksgiving. Out on the New York streets, the noise and agitation of early Christmas shopping are in full ferment. Downstairs in the same building, panicked parents storm FAO Schwarz. Across Fifth Avenue, women crowd the cosmetic counters at Bergdorf Goodman, battling to buy the last lipsticks in holiday color stories that are already all but sold out. For the rest of the world, today is November 20. In Dominique's world, it's sometime next September.

This is the office where each color story starts. This is how each season's seduction begins.

Officially, Dominique is senior vice president of product development at Estée Lauder, flagship brand of the august, multibillion-dollar Estée Lauder corporation. Unofficially, she is its in-house fabulist. Its corporate Scheherazade.

"I don't pick a color and say 'This is the color of the season. Come on everybody, wear it!'" Dominique says, looking fleetingly wistful for the good old days when benevolent despots like Estée Lauder did exactly that. "It's a lot of research. A lot of slaving away."

To make her point, Dominique waves her arms around an office that is earnestly unglamorous. Except for a few forlorn lab samples that look like they might grow up to be eye shadows some day, there isn't any makeup in sight. The west wall has been turned into a big bulletin board. White and off-white fabric swatches are tacked alongside weird close-ups that could double as illustrations to a social anthropology text. In one, white mascara makes a pale young model look like the kind of rabbit Alice must have followed into Wonderland.

Fashion magazines cover the desktop, the small table, chair seats, and sections of the floor. *Madame Figaro, W, Harper's Bazaar. Elle*s from everywhere. *Vogue*s in editions from America, England, France, Germany, Italy, and Spain. Stacks of magazines in Japanese, a language she can't read.

A handsome, voluble Frenchwoman of a certain age, Dominique acts affably oblivious to the trends around her. Her own nails are short and bare. Her makeup is so minimal and so standardized—always the line of hazel on the inside of the lower lid to match the hazel eyes, always the faint stain of lipstick, always the lightest coat of mascara—that it manages to give the impression that she's not wearing any. A former makeup artist, Dominique pretends to be mortified by the suggestion that she would ever vary this maquillage. (At the very thought, her eyes go wide, her mouth forms an O, then her hand flies to her brow.)

She wears a mostly burgundy jacket from Shanghai Tang, a store famous for color combinations that send most other Manhattanites scurrying across Madison Avenue to buy from Barneys' safe black racks. Underneath, she wears a hazel tunic and pants from Issey Miyake, a designer rarely featured in any of the magazines in this office. Her feet are in fancy bedroom slippers from Stubbs & Wootton. Her honey-colored hair is always pinned into a French twist. Always. No one can remember seeing it any other way.

When she talks about her work, Dominique affects an attitude best described as passionate detachment. "Doing this job comes from years after years you are looking at what is going on," she says. "Even then, it does not come to you just like that."

By way of demonstration, she grabs a dog-eared magazine, which falls open to a model who looks like she lost a fight with a housepainter. Dominique gives the page a happy little *thwap!* Perfect for her purposes. That thick swipe of white across the model's forehead? "Eyebrow! Eyebrow!" says Dominique excitedly, pronouncing it "bro" in her strong French accent.

"Who wants to have that?" she asks Socratically, giving the white-swiped model in the magazine another little *thwap.* "Who wants to have that?" Apparently, no one. "But you think 'Oh my God, we have to do something for eyebrow!'"

Thus another beauty trend begins. "You see these runway shows and things and you think 'My God, who wants to have that?' It's not wearable," says Dominique, arching her own elegantly unaugmented brows. "But it gives you a sign. It gives you a direction."

• • •

Actually, by the beauty calendar, the brow thing has come and gone. ("Passé for me," shrugs Dominique, after sounding so gung-ho a minute ago.) Fall is the obsession of the moment.

Big companies—this one included—need about eighteen months to come up with the three or four lipsticks, nail polishes, and eye shadows that constitute the average color story. At its beginning, the story isn't much more than a catchy phrase or a couple of pages clipped from a magazine. In memos and conversations between the company's creative and marketing departments, it's referred to generically, as "spring" or "fall" or "holiday." Finally, toward the end of its first nine months, the story starts to appear on a concept board, a collage of magazine pictures that looks like someone's art therapy.

Only after that long gestation does a story begin its life as makeup. Fabric swatches and magazine pictures and just about anything else the appropriate color—this office once dispatched a jelly bean—are sent off to labs to be transubstantiated into lipsticks and powders. (Like many industries, beauty companies' corporate headquarters are usually miles away from where the products are made.) For this story, Lauder went as far as Europe and as close as its own factory on Long Island. Lab submissions and corrections flurried back and forth until jobbed-out pans of color and the homemade stuff had a recognizable relationship.

That's where Dominique is today: The color story

has a working title and a range of product samples that look pretty much like what will end up on store counters next August. In ten days, it will be whisked away to the factory for good. By next month, it will be rolling off the production line.

Like any genre, the color story has its own conventions. It must be topical and trendy, but it cannot be exclusionary or over specific. As applied to lipstick, that means at least one shade that's pale, one that's completely crazy, and one that's neutral. Something for everyone. "We try to find colors to be at the trend or at the spirit of the moment," she explains, "but that everyone can still find her shade." A good color story gives women a chance to get away—without going too far.

To add an element of suspense, Dominique varies the total number of products. If one season reads as a Tolstoyan saga, the next will look terse and modernist.

She also puts a plot twist, what the industry calls a "kicker," in every story. A kicker is the beauty department's novelty item. The mink teddy bear. The diamond tennis bracelet. The splendidly silly thing that nobody needs and everybody wants. Back in Bellevue Square Mall, it was the turquoise mascara. "Kicker is not very important, but a little bit crazy," she says, "because it's in and out—to attract not only the press but the customer."

Finally, a good story should have the pacing of a thriller. "Those colors are in and out. They don't stay, so there is a need to see them," Dominique explains.

"That urgency to buy the product because women know it will disappear." Each story stays on counter a month or two at most (if it sells out). Or until the next one comes along (if it doesn't).

Once upon a time, there was a mighty empress named Estée.

She and her consort gave birth to two princes, who grew up to have princes and princesses of their own. Under the wise stewardship of the crown prince, Estée's empire grew and grew. Eventually, it boasted over a dozen kingdoms, each covering so much territory that Estée's original brand, that stalwart stronghold for so many years, began to look forlorn and forgotten.

At long last, just when serious lack of chic threatened to do away with its market dominance, a young heroine appeared who vowed to return the family's first brand to its former splendor. This was none other than Estée's own granddaughter. Aerin Lauder Zinterhofer. It Girl. Bright Young Thing. Park Avenue Princess *sans pareil*.

Like a real-life version of the heroine in that fairy tale about the princess and the pea, Aerin came to her task possessed of an uncanny inborn ability to detect the single chic shade buried in a tray of seemingly similar lab samples. As well as the innate authority to unhesitatingly banish the entire tray of samples back to the lab for a fifth, sixth, or seventh go-round.

Nor were such wondrous talents confined to cosmetics. Fairies bending over her cradle blessed her with a fashion sense that made her copied everywhere she went. At a tender age, Aerin exhibited enough of a trademark style—sexier than her socialite set, less studied than the trying-too-hard career girls—to get herself photographed at all the best bashes in New York and Palm Beach. Paeans to her predilection for high-heeled Manolo Blahniks were published by fawning fashion magazines far and wide.

This is what she wears to work on a very cold Friday in late November: a cobalt-blue cashmere sweater ("My mother got if for me about two years ago. It's old."), which plays off that huge cornflower-blue sapphire in her engagement ring; snug, gray, boot-cut pants purchased on a shopping expedition with the beauty editor of *Harper's Bazaar;* three-and-a-half-inch stiletto-heeled Manolo Blahnik sandals; and a man's steel Rolex. Already enveloped in enchantment as she is, Aerin appears to feel little need for makeup and is notorious for not wearing any. At present, her chief cosmetic enhancement is the pearly polish on the perfect toenails framed by the gray lizard of those $695 Manolos.

Coming to the family empire straight out of school, Aerin met each challenge put before her until, at last, she proved herself worthy of the title Director of Creative Product Development, a catchall that means she has a smaller, similarly decorated office next door to

Dominique's, that she goes on advertising shoots to ensure that they convey what she calls "the Estée Lauder lifestyle" (which appears to be identical to her own), and that she weighs in on assorted matters of taste (like packaging, supervising stylists, or hiring photographers).

Now, however, she must once again prove her mettle by assisting in the company's quest for a fall color story, a trial that may tax her magical reserves of good taste like nothing before.

Already, this is not shaping up to be a particularly easy season. Noblesse oblige.

If you've ever wondered why everybody in the fashion industry gets fixated on the same things at the same time, the short answer is Première Vision.

A biannual textile trade show in Villepinte, just outside Paris, Première Vision promises nothing less than a glimpse into the future. Attend and you find out what you'll be wearing next year, what you'll be eating, and where you'll be going on vacation. The March edition shows the world as it will be the following spring. October shows the next year's fall.

Big, slick, and bilingual, the show has long since become a self-fulfilling prophecy. All the big stores, fashion houses, and beauty companies attend. So all of them invest according to the information they get at the show. All the designers start next year's collections with the fabric they find there, thus guaranteeing that stores are always full of whatever Première Vision predicted.

This sounds sort of glamorous, until you arrive in Villepinte. There you see what fashion can be like without models, makeup, or music: A huge trade show split into eight hundred little booths, most of them displaying fabric swatches mounted on boards or stapled to little hangers. With buyers and browsers—41,615 of them at the show Aerin and Dominique attended a month ago—wandering from booth to booth fingering fabrics and writing orders.

In theory, anybody can pay $25 to get into Première Vision. In practice, nobody outside the business would want to. Although the occasional presentation is elaborate (e.g., the fiber exhibition that employed a trapeze artist, a storyteller, and a clown), most are strange pictures surrounded by swatches of fabric and swathes of color. The good ones are evocative. The bad ones are baffling.

Written explanations aren't much help. Imagine the most pretentious fashion prose you've ever read overlaid with deconstructivist analysis and then translated from the French. For example, the official theme for fall was "Tropism," explained thusly: "For the first winter of the third millennium, Tropism is the meeting point of unexpected marriages, functional connections, and sophistication liberated from nostalgic textiles attached to the past."

Dominique, who's been through dozens of these,

walked October's show the way she always does: look-ing, touching, watching videos. She makes a point of not taking notes. Nor does she sketch, take Polaroids, dictate into a tape recorder, or delegate any of those du-ties to an assistant. "I never take a note. Never, never. Which makes people mad at me because it's not Ameri-can thinking."

She also studies the other attendees, the fashion groupies, the students who do the menial jobs. "They carry the trend on themselves. The trend may be very ugly . . . but in two years it will be on the streets." And whenever she makes one of these trips, Dominique brings poetry, usually in French, to read on the plane—as a break from her steady diet of fashion magazines.

This time she saw lots of thick, textured fabrics, which means thick, textured clothes were on their way. She saw mohair and boiled cashmere. She saw the same wintry whites that were already on her office wall. She saw plums and grays. She noticed a tendency to pair red with green. She flipped through packets of color chips. But that was just an exercise. She knew right away which color was important. She just knew.

Her competitors knew too. "We are all in the same range of shades because we go to the same place. We have the same information. We read the same books," she says with a shrug. There's no escaping it.

The color of the season is going to be gray.

•   •   •

"It's like when you make up a story for a young child and you have to make up all the different characters and plot," Aerin says, as she pulls out a big piece of cardboard covered with little swatches of cloth and pictures cut out of magazines. This is Estée Lauder's fall story.

Aerin started working on this about nine months ago. Like a high-bred hunting dog sniffing the wind, she sat through runway shows, did due diligence with trend forecasts, and studied textiles. Sitting at the round table in Dominique's office, she points to an old clipping from *Women's Wear Daily*, the trade paper that is Holy Writ for both the beauty and fashion industries: "I rip this out and it's talking about the importance of mohair and cashmere and how people want luxury but they want it to be comfortable."

That forecast, broad as a bad horoscope, led Aerin to designer sneakers. These were about luxury and comfort, too. Aerin knew that those were another sign. At this stage, no one was worried too much about translating the designer sneakers into makeup. "It's information," Dominique chimes in, "and it's a culture."

The clothes her lipsticks and eye shadows are supposed to complement wouldn't be around for at least a year. They weren't even on the drawing boards yet. So she cut "swipe," meaning pictures already published someplace else. Then, when she had a folder full, she started to look for recurring themes.

After about six months of this, Aerin was ready to start the storyboard she's holding now. No beauty products appear on the cardboard, which is as gorgeously glum as an Ingmar Bergman movie. Desolate beaches are its dominant image. When people appear, they are aloof and alone. Skies are overcast. Colors are muted.

On those bleak horizons, Aerin saw green-grays and brown-grays that might make nice eye shadows. Among those monotonous rocks, she spotted purple-grays with plenty of lipstick potential. She named the story "Winter Beach." In Aerin's story, dull skies speak of Nordic influences, misanthropic models are in the midst of romantic reveries, and dingy colors communicate nostalgia.

"You're yearning for something you don't have," says Aerin. "Here it's not cold anymore. There's never snow," she adds, making it sound like the models are melancholy about the impact of global warming. "That's why the whole winter beach feeling is very appealing. Because it's something you don't have anymore."

The fabric swatches attached to her board are all nubby and matted. Even the most opulent, a piece of metallic lace, looks tarnished. The swatch of boiled cashmere doesn't look luxurious, it looks like what's left of an old sweater after it's been through the wash too many times. Looking at the storyboard, it's hard to imagine anyone yearning for anything on it.

Dominique, who's done dozens of these storyboards herself, beams at Aerin's handiwork. She brings her hands together in a soundless clap and exclaims, "I love the whole thing!"

Aerin starts to explain, but both women are so keen on "Winter Beach" that they complete each other's sentences. "The importance of gray . . ."

"Grayish-greenish . . ." adds Dominique, standing to point to a particularly bleak patch of picture.

" . . . is continuous."

"You see a lot of green in that gray," declares Dominique, now knee-deep in nuance. "Also a lot of different white and stone and sand and wood on the beach and stuff like that."

Then they come to the swatches. "Very often the fabric dictates the texture of our product. Meaning when you see a lot of satin fabrics, you know you have to put that trend in your product as shine. So, when you see all this mohair . . ."

"It's going to be soft."

"Like cashmere. It has to be soft—a little matted, though."

"Like a very moisturizing lipstick would work for this," says Aerin, pointing to a patch of coarsely woven fabric that resembles nothing less than a very moisturizing lipstick.

Aerin pauses, gestures graciously in the direction of her storyboard, and sums up the entire exercise by saying: "You learn not to think so literally."

• • •

Around here, they make it sound like Estée Lauder invented the color story. "She was the one who did that in such a big way that it was phenomenal in the stores," says Dominique with some pride. And taking credit for them would have been just like Estée. But color stories were going strong for at least a decade before Estée arrived on the scene.

After World War I, beauty companies still had to battle to make lipstick and rouge socially acceptable. The rise of Hollywood helped a lot: More and more women wanted to look like the stars they saw in movies, who obviously did some dipping into the paint pots.

Advertising also advanced the cause. Early copywriters made makeup sound like a sacred trust: It was the God-given right—and obligation!—of the American woman to improve herself. In her 1920 ads, a Polish immigrant named Helena Rubinstein co-opted the Puritan work ethic and made it the foundation of the American beauty industry by penning admonishments like: "Self-satisfaction is twin brother to the pea-cock. Whatever is done can be done better." A 1926 ad for Armand face powder followed a similar line: "Yesterday's plain women are today smart-looking! They have faced their mirrors frankly. 'I am not good-looking,' they say, 'but I can look interesting!' So—with exquisite grooming and a smart make-up—they achieve their own striking type."

Makeup was also endorsed by early advocates of women's rights, something contemporary feminists like to forget. Seventy years before Naomi Wolf came along to decry the cult-like techniques of cosmetics sales in *The Beauty Myth*, suffragettes and their immediate successors wore lipstick as a badge of liberation. Painting your face meant writing your own story, independent of whatever your husband or father had plotted for you. Makeup was a hard-won privilege, like voting or holding a job. Besides, seeing makeup on a "nice" girl irritated the hell out of most men.

Meanwhile, women's media was also busily promoting beauty, which was turning out to be a nice, steady source of both readership and ad revenue. Makeup, they told women time and time again, was modern. "Smart" women, in the days when that adjective also meant fashionable, wore lipstick.

Painting your lips no longer made you a floozy, no more than showing your ankles or learning to type. Matrons, churchwomen, college students, secretaries, and socialites could buy cosmetics now. Wearing lipstick and powder was socially sanctioned as something conscientious and clever. It showed that you wanted to make something of yourself.

Beauty became the tenth largest business in the United States during the 1920s. By the end of the decade, Sears, Roebuck and Co. sold more face powder than soap. Sales kept increasing during the Great Depression (as they would during subsequent wars, depressions, and disasters). Up until this point, cosmetics companies had only to expand their audience to expand their business. Now that the market was more saturated, they had to come up with some other way to keep profits pouring in.

It didn't take long. Before the 1930s were far gone, the industry "educated" women to all kinds of niceties. Not every shade was suitable for every complexion. Not every shade was suitable for every ensemble. Evening makeup had to be different from daytime makeup (which doubled the amount a woman was supposed to own), and spring or summer makeup had to be different from fall or winter makeup (which doubled it again). Makeup's power of expression was increasing exponentially.

Enter the color story. Since last season's lipstick could not possibly express the mood of the moment, collections with fashion tie-ins and cute names began appearing each fall and spring. For example, in September 1939—the season that taupe was trendy and bustles were here to stay—Elizabeth Arden (who claimed *she* invented the color story) advertised "Burnt Sugar" as the makeup that "belongs on every woman's lips and fingertips when she wears the browns, the taupes, and high-fashion beiges." The next year—when bustles looked tired and anything American Indian was chic— fall makeup had names like "Indian Love Call" and "Wigwam."

French fashion designer Germaine Monteil (who claimed *she* invented the color story) supposedly got into the beauty business because she couldn't find the correct lipstick shades to complement her seasonal dress collections. Her first lipstick came out in 1936. By 1942, the makeup line was so lucrative that she dropped the dress collections.

By the time Revlon started doing them in 1944, spring and fall color stories were as much a harbinger of the season as Easter bonnets or back-to-school shopping. "Pink Lightning." "Plumb Beautiful." "Where's the Fire?" "Paint the Town Pink." Founder Charles Revson (who claimed *he* invented the color story) ran ads that were big, glossy, and luscious to look at. No sermons. Only glorious overstatement. "Fatal Apple . . . the most tempting color since Eve winked at Adam." The new style of advertising worked so well that Revlon kept using it. So did everyone else. Fashion magazines, which had been obligingly grinding out gushy editorial about their beauty advertisers since the 1920s, were pressured for still more mentions if they wanted to keep Revlon's business. You would have had to live in a cave to escape annunciations of Revlon's "Cherries in the Snow" or "Fire and Ice."

By the 1950s, cosmetics were second only to food in sheer volume of advertising. And not only in print. On TV, Revlon rival Hazel Bishop sponsored *This Is Your Life* while Revlon owned *The $64,000 Question*, although both shows were black and white and both companies based their business on color.

The ante kept going up. In an industry where it was already axiomatic that all advertising be aspirational—

why buy a lipstick unless it's going to change your appearance?—color stories swelled into escapist extravaganzas. Estée Lauder, a woman with a pronounced personal fondness for fancy dress and formal entertaining, produced the equivalent of MGM musicals long after MGM had gotten out of the fantasy-for-the-masses business.

Few, if any, of her ads deigned to display product. One season, L'Oréal's advertising showed Brussels Sprout eye shadow, Chili Chile lipstick, and Au Currant nail polish. For that same season, Lauder presented "Venetian Court Colors," an epic of goofy grandiloquence that depicted majestically gowned and jeweled house model Karen Graham posed inside real Renaissance palazzos and wafting along the Grand Canal. In the Lauder version, the story was clearly more important than the color. Makeup didn't even make it onto the page.

Color stories were both breaking news and style commandments, much as hemlines had once been. "We could put whatever . . . and you *had* to do that. Otherwise? *Pfff!*"—Dominique waves her hand to dismiss those who dared disregard the dictates—"Women rushed to the store. It was 'Oh, it's the fashion, they say you *have* to wear it.'"

Lauder would jet assorted executives and hired guns to Greece or some other off-season, exotic backdrop for a no-expense-spared photo spectacular. "It was a *huge* event!" Dominique recalls. "We had thirty persons flying first class to Greece. Or the desert. Or Florida. We had the photographer, the model, the makeup artistes, the hairdresser, the people in charge . . ."

Then, a heartbeat later, the whole thing was over. Passé. "Suddenly it was *Pfff!*"—another gesture of Gallic dismissal—"I don't care what they say!" The beauty industry was going to do without color stories from now on.

Out with capricious inspiration! In with social service! Career looks covered counters. The trend was to pretend you didn't follow trends. One company launched "The Nakeds," makeup you wore to pretend you didn't wear makeup. Makeup artists started their own lines. Bobbi Brown called hers the Essentials, implying that the colors would not be automatically outdated each season.

That got old fast. Nakeds and basics and essentials weren't much fun to buy or wear. And why stop by the beauty counter if there's never going to be anything new? Why go to the beauty department at all if it's going to be as boring as the sock department?

Women wanted the fantasy back, thank you very much.

So color stories came back. Highly paid executives painted their fingernails blue and carpooling moms put sparkles on their skin. The new, no-nonsense beauty companies churned out glittery products. Lauder started advertising its stories again—albeit calling them "shade statements" to try to sound more hip.

The big difference between now and the old days is that those fabulous, faraway photo shoots are over. Instead of jetting off somewhere exotic to shoot "Winter Beach," the Estée Lauder model will pose in a New York studio the week after next. Aerin will supervise. While they're both there, the company will piggyback campaigns for future stories (then retouch the pictures in a year or two when it's time for them to run). As Aerin says: "You can create almost anything with all the technology that we have."

The phantasmagoria has been taken down a notch or two. Backdrops are less specific. Now every woman who comes to the counter can put herself in the picture.

For spring, the story was pink. That was an easy one. Pink is flattering. Pink is feminine. Pink is upbeat. Pink is easy to sell.

Fall does not look so rosy. Gray is not flattering. Gray is not feminine. Gray is not upbeat. Gray is not easy to sell. And, as if all that wasn't bad enough, gray was the color of the season last year too.

"I've done pink twice. I've done gray. I've done this. I've done that," says Aerin, with a world weariness way beyond her years. She lets out a long slow breath that stops just short of being a sigh. "Sometimes it's really hard."

Every beauty company runs into this problem. Each solves it a slightly different way. Some consult makeup artists or commission their own trend forecasts. Others go further afield for their aesthetic epiphanies. Partly for prestige, partly so the competition won't get the same thing. Aerin and Dominique use books, movies, or whatever strikes their fancy. This time they included the "Millet/van Gogh" exhibit at the Musée d'Orsay in Paris.

Art with more antipathy to the beauty industry would have been hard to find. Gallery after gallery showed peasants who looked like potatoes wearing clothes the color of dirt. The van Gogh in this show was not the Vincent of the brilliant Provençal palette and the popular *Sunflowers* and *Starry Night*. This was the severe, sermonizing van Gogh of the dreary, dun palette and the emphatically unpretty people. The van Gogh who copied Jean François Millet's paintings of farmers toiling like beasts of burden. The van Gogh who conferred his highest praise on Millet by writing: "Is not life given us to become richer in spirit, even though the outward appearance may suffer?"

The Lauder team could not have been more thrilled. "The tints and the color are exactly what is going on now," Dominique exclaims happily. "The mood in the tableaux—about this worker, with earth, with water—was very important for us." From Dominique's perspective, it was practically a straight line from *The Angelus* to eye shadow. From Dominique's perspective, it all comes down to beauty in the end.

. . .

Gray.

After all their aesthetic epiphanies and trend reports and trips to trade shows, Aerin and Dominique are still stuck with gray.

Gray brings out the color of no one's eyes. Gray is impossible for a blusher. Gray can look deathly as a nail polish. And gray lipstick, although it's been done before, is just not an Estée Lauder shade. It's hard to imagine even Aerin being able to pull it off. Not to the birthday blowout for two of her Upper East Side chums which she'll attend tonight and which will be documented on the society page of *Women's Wear Daily* next week. Certainly not to the New York Botanical Garden's Winter Wonderland Ball, which she co-chairs next month and which will be duly documented in *WWD, The New York Times, Vogue,* and every other place that matters. No, gray is just not a shade you can slap on your spokesmodel and expect to sell.

But Estée didn't build her empire by letting a little thing like that stop her, and her granddaughter is not about to start now. Gray doesn't sell? Pink does? Then turn gray into pink.

Aerin holds up a card from a trend forecasting service, which is headlined "Platinum." No one acquainted with the practice of trend forecasting will be surprised to learn that there is not a single platinum-colored thing on the card. The little twists of yarn attached to it are all pink.

Some are very vivid, the kinds of colors that beauty copy-writers like to call fuchsia and clematis and cyclamen.

"You will see four beautiful lipsticks with high, high sheen like that," says Dominique, gesturing toward the yarn twists, which have no sheen whatsoever. "It's not so gray and dull. It's a beautiful balance. But it's a very quiet palette." Reaching out to stroke the little yarn twists with a fingertip, Dominique looks like she has fallen for the story already.

Aerin produces a piece of cardboard with lab samples glued to it, the working model of "Winter Beach." Nothing here is gray either.

The eye shadows seem sort of greenish, sort of brownish. The blush is pink. The lipsticks look mauve. They are all, as Dominique puts it, "quiet."

But maybe this isn't the whole story. "Yesterday we were still adding a color that we *love.* That mauvy-beigy lipstick," Dominique adds eagerly, her phrases coming out faster and faster as she looks over the lab samples. "I think we want to play with that color, add more, find something else, come up with another idea. . . ."

This means that, even though "Winter Beach" has to be in final formula in ten days, at least one more round of submissions and revisions will go back and forth between here and the company's lipstick lab on Long Island.

"Winter Beach" is only a working title: Last year, "Seashell" was renamed "Amazing Greys" after the marketing department got hold of it. Products can still be added and dropped. For all the nine months of planning, a lot of other things could happen between now and the time this ends up on counter.

Seduction doesn't always go as planned. Moods change without warning, reliable ploys fall spectacularly flat. The dozen long-stemmed roses turn into a cliché. The pricey box of confections suddenly seems cloying despite so many years as a sure-fire thing.

Dominique's record in these matters is better than most. Like Scheherazade, she beguiles well enough to keep herself in business. If "Winter Beach" works out, she'll spin or supervise another one, and if that one works too, there'll be more after it. Another audience to enthrall. Another spring and fall. Another story and another.

When Dominique was imported to take the job at Lauder in 1991, she came fresh from a big success at Guerlain. Until she started its makeover, cosmetics made by that venerable French perfume house had been looking a little too venerable for fashionable taste. She changed that.

She invented liquid eyeliners in silver and gold. She swanked up the packaging, putting blusher into tiny, domed compacts so absolutely adorable that women doted on them even though the colors inside were nothing new. She invented Météorites, a candy box filled with pastel powders compressed into shiny spheres that looked like delectable, if inedible, bonbons. Women had no idea what to do with Météorites, but it was so beautiful that they bought it anyway.

Once she got to Lauder, she invented a blusher inside a *tourbillion*, a pretty toy that whirled on a vanity table like a spinning top. Inside its lid was an ingenious full-sized brush to swirl around the whorls of powder in the bottom.

But her top flopped. "In Europe, in Japan, in Asia, it was a huge success," she remembers. "Not here." Alas, that was the season of the serious auteur. Americans fell for pared-down packaging. Bare-bones makeup artists' lines became the darlings of the beauty press. Whimsy was out.

Not long after, Dominique did a story called "Purple Reign," which was an all-purple epic encompassing plum, lavender, mauve, and one lipstick in the same blue-violet that comes out of a Bic ballpoint.

That was a huge hit.

She shrugs. "Sometimes you can do the most incredible collection and you don't know why it doesn't work." The trips to Première Vision, the trend forecasting, the fussing, and the back-and-forth to the lab are the same for each color story, each year. Sometimes the results inspire ardor in the press and passionate consumption at the counter, and sometimes they lay an egg. In the empire of Estée Lauder, every story has a happy ending, but some are happier than others. Last season's story, for example, earned well enough internationally, but was no runaway hit in the home market.

This one could go either way. Some seasons women want fairy tales. Some seasons they crave adventure. As Dominique has learned all too well. Leaning over the lab samples and looking again at the wistful, romantic pictures on the "Winter Beach" storyboard, she says "You know, we are not just selling makeup."

December

MANUFACTURING: THE MOTHER
OF INVENTION

Happy Holidays!

All during December, counters are a blur of fast-moving merchandise. Perfume sets. Limited-edition compacts. Glittery body powders. Gifts with purchase. Color stories spun solely for the short-lived glory of seasonal celebration. Paint your lips gold. Powder your lids platinum. Believe that beauty advisor who tells you metallics are a must. Turn yourself into a Christmas tree.

Women who know better, women who never do this sort of thing, indulge in the grooming equivalent of getting loaded at the office Christmas party. Soccer moms deck themselves with sparkles. Corporate lawyers get batting practice with false eyelashes. And teenagers, who've been wearing all of that stuff all along, get a chance to really go to town. Right in front of their parents.

Tidings of great joy!

The season of infinite promise and unrealistic expectations is here, and with it, beauty's biggest profits. The holidays are the industry's chance to kick back and celebrate. Fall stories are safely delivered to the factories. No one has to worry about the wild card of runway shows for another two months. Advertising and sales training are tabled for the time being. And cosmetic sales have gone up yet again this year.

In the media, Aerin swans through society pages, fawned over as "The Girl Most Invited." Andrea Jung, the head of Avon, appears in endless business stories, a token female in a company man's world. Erica Kane, the soap opera makeup mogul played by Susan Lucci, reigns as America's daytime heroine. Bobbi Brown, Trish McEvoy, Laura Mercier, and newly minted makeup millionaires are a staple of inspirational articles and TV segments. Everywhere you look, success is all mixed up with beauty.

Hallelujah!

In makeup, a medium without permanence, a woman can write and rewrite her story as often as she likes.

Cosmetics change lives. Not just by distracting a disaffected housewife. Or giving a woman a new look for her new job. Or diverting a couple of overscheduled soccer moms. Cosmetics make women rich and powerful.

Back in the days when few women entered business, cosmetics made multimillionaires of Helena Rubinstein, Elizabeth Arden, and Estée Lauder. Over decades, history repeated itself dozens and dozens of times. Along the way, men started beauty companies too. But this was one business where men could never take over as the main attraction, the star of the show. Not in the same way.

Beauty history sounds like Horatio Alger rewritten for women. Central to each tale is the heroine's unshakeable belief in her product and herself. Instead of waiting around for her knight in shining armor, each plucky heroine overcomes enormous odds by dint of good old-fashioned guts and hard work. Each happy ending rewards her with exquisite art, gracious homes, glittering jewelry, closets full of couture, and all else that her heart has ever desired.

The ineluctable moral of each story: When a woman goes to the beauty counter, she enters a world where—armed with enough work and just the right product—she can reshape life to her liking.

Born in Poland on December 25, 1872, Helena Rubinstein was the oldest of eight girls. Supposedly, her father wanted her to study medicine. Helena liked the lab work well enough, but had no plans to spend the rest of her days around unattractive sick people. With future in Cracow looking less than lovely, Helena packed her bags to visit a branch of the family that had emigrated to Australia. A farm in the Outback wasn't much to her liking either. So Helena moved to Melbourne, the nearest metropolis.

Her mother had shipped her Down Under with twelve jars of the family's favorite face cream, which, together with her own comely complexion, made her a beauty expert in a city full of weathered, worn-out frontierswomen. Soon she was trying to parlay her face cream into her fortune and sending home for more jars. Helena borrowed £250 and spent half on the product from Poland (which she promptly repackaged under her own label) and the other half in setting up a skin care salon. She told everyone her product was concocted of herbs, almonds, and evergreens. It wasn't, but she had a genius for knowing what women wanted to hear.

Her break came when a newspaper write-up resulted in fifteen thousand orders. Helena, or "Madame" as she was henceforth known, sent home for help. Two sisters and the man who made the cream were dispatched to Australia. By 1907, she was in London. By 1912, she was in Paris. When World War I broke out in Europe, she decided to conquer America. While all of this was going on, she married and gave birth to two sons. The three of them didn't slow her down a bit.

By the time the war was over, Madame had coast-to-coast American salons and was selling in department stores. When women came for skin care, it was easy to sell them makeup too. First powder and lipstick and rouge. Then, in imitation of movie stars, theatrical makeup like mascara and kohl and eye shadow—repackaged under her own name.

Using massive amounts of money, art, and jewelry to bulldoze barriers to Jews, immigrants, and working women, Madame got to know everyone from Matisse to Marlene Dietrich. She was a pal of Picasso's, a patroness of Salvador Dalí. Cocteau called her "the Empress of Beauty." It was the perfect title. She had a Napoleonic personality, a bizarrely imperial dress sense that ran to stuffs like sable and Somali leopard, and she routinely used the royal "we" in casual conversation. At four feet, ten inches, Madame was larger than life. For years she reigned as the richest self-made woman in the world.

She died at age ninety-two, having outlived two husbands and a son, and having failed to establish a strong line of succession. Her empire changed hands several times, each time becoming more dowdy and downmarket, until it ended up at L'Oréal, the French cosmetics conglomerate that recently brought it back to New York as a boutique brand, a one-time world power turned into a chic resort destination.

The second member of the industry's foundation trilogy didn't learn any lessons from her archrival's end, since she outlived Madame by only a year. Born Florence Nightingale Graham to Canadian truck farmers on December 31, 1878, Elizabeth Arden never finished high school. She tried nursing school and dropped out because, like Madame, she couldn't abide the appearance of sick people. Eventually, she got herself to New York and a job in a beauty salon. In 1910, still unmarried, she borrowed $6,000 from her brother, rechristened herself Mrs. Elizabeth Arden, and opened her own salon. With the same logic that would characterize subsequent business decisions, she then announced she wished to be known as "Miss Arden."

Like Madame, Miss Arden did not marry and become an American citizen until age thirty-seven. Like Madame, she divorced her American first husband and chose a Russian prince as his successor. Also like Madame, she tried to conquer the world, up to and including Berlin, one of the few capitals her Jewish compatriot had not aggressively annexed. (Hitler tried to make makeup *verboten*, but everyone from Eva Braun to the Mitford sisters wore lipstick anyway. Frau Hermann Göring was a particular fan of the Arden salon.)

In 1934, Miss Arden founded Maine Chance, effectively starting the spa business in America. The secret to a spa, she maintained, was putting women in a setting where they became utterly infantile and self-absorbed. She saw it as a natural extension of her other beauty business. When she wasn't selling, the childless Miss Arden raced thoroughbreds—her "babies." Her Maine Chance stables were an obsession equivalent to Madame's art acquisitions, and actually produced a

Kentucky Derby winner in 1946. Her racing silks were nursery pink and baby blue, the same colors as her packaging.

Well into her ninth decade, the five-foot-two-inch Miss Arden was prone to girlish hissy fits of hiring and firing. When she died in 1966, the tax mess took years to straighten out. The spas went first, then most of the salons. Her company changed hands until it ended up as a subsidiary of Unilever, her one-time world power gone the way of Attila the Hun's.

The surviving member of the triumvirate, Estée Lauder, attended Miss Arden's memorial service on the arm of her son—a neat symbol of why her empire did not end up like the other two. Estée always knew how to keep her family close and employ them to advantage.

Josephine Esther Mentzer was born on July 1, 1908, in Corona, Queens, the daughter of Hungarian immigrants. She graduated high school, and got married to the son of Austrian immigrants a couple of years later. She became Estée by prettifying Esther, her middle name, and Lauder by prettifying Lauter, her married name. Like Madame and Miss Arden, Estée also divorced her first husband. Unlike them, she remarried him.

Like them, she also started in skin care, in her case pushing creams cooked up by an uncle in a converted stable. She soon progressed to a restaurant on West Sixty-fourth Street, where she and her husband, Joe, would stay up all night brewing beauty potions in the kitchen. While Joe stayed behind the scenes, Estée hawked product. She later liked to claim that it was at about this time that she invented "gift with a purchase," her industry's equivalent of a bartender saying, "This round's on the house."

Her career in color cosmetics began when she went to a jobber and got turquoise eye shadow and red lipstick to sell alongside the skin care. Her first break came in the late 1940s when she got a counter at Saks Fifth Avenue. Estée sent engraved invitations, worked the counter herself, and sold out in two days.

The next break was her 1953 invention of Youth-Dew, an odoriferous liquid that she insisted on labeling bath oil. Estée wanted women to buy and wear scent for themselves instead of waiting for a man to give it to them—something that sounded less political if her product wasn't actually called perfume. As it turned out, American women were more than ready to give themselves a little treat. After Youth-Dew, Estée had them hooked.

For the next decade or so, Estée's own story seemed like a twentieth-century retelling of Silas Lapham, the fictional hero whose attempt to change from self-made paint merchant into Boston Brahmin was meant to be a cautionary tale about overweening ambition. Snooty bluebloods, who joyfully scooped up the products she donated to charity events, snickered that she used free lipsticks to get chummy with the Begum Aga Khan and the Duchess of Windsor. Catty editors, who flattered her as a Viennese aristocrat in the articles they ran next to her ads, slagged her as an uppity Jew when her back was turned.

But little Estée was made of sterner stuff than any Silas, and she made overweening ambition into a moral imperative. As business got better and better, she threw more parties, bought more couture, acquired more art, made more donations to charity. She smiled her way through more society events, gave away more goody bags to more catty editors, converted more customers at more in-store appearances. Her husband stood right by her side and she secured her line of succession: Both sons work in her company, as do both their wives, and three out of the four grandchildren. Including the tall, slim, socially ubiquitous Aerin.

These days, Lauder stock may be publicly traded, but 77 percent of the company remains "privately" (read "largely family") held, and the empire founded by the nervy little blonde from Queens vies for international industry domination: spinning off Clinique, Prescriptives, and Origins; annexing Bobbi Brown Essentials, Aveda, M·A·C, and a dozen others.

Listen to enough stories like that, and the idea of using a little lipstick to reinvent yourself is an easy sell.

It's still possible for anybody to start a beauty company. No prior experience needed.

Say you wake up one morning and decide to become a beauty mogul. Your first step will be joining a trade organization like ICMAD (Independent Cosmetic Manufacturers & Distributors), which will cost you about $300 and get you a regional directory of suppliers.

Open your directory and you'll discover that only the big guns own factories—Avon, Lauder, Mary Kay, Maybelline, Revlon, and their ilk. Most of the industry makes do with the same network of suppliers that you're going to be using. There's also lots and lots of overlap, since even the biggest beauty companies have to get their specialty components from somewhere. Certain suppliers hold mini-monopolies. That means you'll probably be buying your mascara brushes from the same Vermont factory that rolls them out for Cover Girl, Estée Lauder, Revlon, and everybody else. And that your pencils or crayons will probably be made by Schwan-STABILO, a company that's been making art supplies forever and beauty supplies for almost as long.

Since those specialists have subspecialties, you'll see that the business gets very arcane very quickly. Not only are there "fillers" (factories that put one company's product in another company's container without adding anything themselves), there's a subcategory of fillers who specialize in teensy sample sizes. Another that specializes in samples that squirt and spray. And so on. Huge companies have entire engineering departments devoted to costing out this kind of stuff.

So, while it's nice to start your company with a specific product in mind, don't be daunted. Sometimes it's easier to hit the trade shows and get a "turnkey" product, then slap your name on it as it comes off the assembly line.

Skip the small-time trade shows. Sign up for the two biggies: Cosmoprof, in Bologna, Italy, in April, and HBA, in New York City in June. They'll give you an overview of the industry and let you pick up a little of the lingo: You are about to enter the world where there is no small or large, only "size impression." A pretty eye shadow is no longer pretty, it has "pan appeal." You won't want to embarrass yourself by mentioning lip pencils or eye pencils; from here on, they're "cosmetic writing instruments."

Cosmoprof is fun. It's beauty's equivalent to Première Vision. Over 100,000 people attend and the big companies put on all kinds of dog and pony shows for them. Most suppliers and visitors are European, but English is the lingua franca, so it's easy for Americans to do business. Plus, if you haven't got a good idea for packaging, you can beg, borrow, or steal one at Cosmopack, a sideshow to the main event. HBA may not be as warm or welcoming. (Mana Products, the Queens-based factory that usually takes a big front booth, can make you feel like something that should be scraped off a shoe.) But dealing with Americans saves you the hassle of importing.

Here, as in most other business, the trick is getting

yourself a reasonable cost of goods. Maybe you remember reading that Urban Decay nail polish initially cost less than $1 to make, went to stores for $6, and sold for $11. That nail polish thing is long since played out, but you'll be shopping for that same cost ratio. Best not to get too greedy at this stage. Forget those stories you've heard about all lipsticks costing $1 to manufacture. (You know those can't be right: Some lipsticks *sell* for 99 cents.)

Big orders reduce your cost of goods. Little orders make it high. As you walk the show floor and ask about minimum orders, you find that three thousand units per product gets laughs, and five thousand, which sounds like a lot to you, is beneath the notice of your new friends. When you bandy bigger numbers, you become more popular.

With any luck, you get a couple of suppliers ready to meet you halfway. Checking them out isn't going to be easy. Nobody in your new business is very forthcoming about problems with suppliers; they're too busy wishing the same problems on you. So you ask around, look around, and order the FDA inspection report (more about that later). Also remember that you'll have to book time on the factory production line at least two months in advance of when you want to start shipping, and then you have to figure in at least a few more weeks to ship. To save time, ask your factory for a large batch of samples, so you can drum up plenty of press before your product exists.

At this point, you'll hire one of the half dozen PR agencies in New York that specializes in beauty. The agency coaches you on how to schmooze beauty editors, what gifts to buy them, and where to wine and dine them. You soon discover that the press is not a cheap date but, with magazine ads costing upward of $40,000 per page, it's still cheaper than advertising.

As magazine raves appear and more stores start wanting your product, you can depend on having all the traditional distribution problems. Like keeping popular colors in stock. And dumping duds in a business that doesn't run sales (more about selling your stuff on television later).

Since your sales are soon passing $4 million or so, you next have to contemplate going global. By then there will be a big multinational fish, like Lauder or LVMH or L'Oréal or Shiseido, waiting to gobble a little fish like you. Although you really don't have to worry about acquisitions for a year or two.

For now, you're on your way.

No vast *Charlie and the Chocolate Factory*–style vats of magic here. Lipsticks are cooked in oversized kettles— no color visible—that look like pressure cookers for a prison cafeteria. Surroundings are spartan and as clean as they need to be.

You'd never guess it, but this is one of the best-known factories in the business. Suffern, an hour north of Man-

hattan, is where the mighty international Avon Corporation concocts its "first to market" innovations. They
boast that the kettles here go all the way up to a thousand gallons, although most look to be in the thirty- to
fifty-gallon range. Quantities that seem like baby
batches for such a big company, until you remember
that a lipstick is only about 3.6 grams, less than an
eighth of an ounce, and that a full-sized eye shadow
weighs less than a gram.

A few months back, when Estée Lauder and everyone else in the industry was doing the same thing,
Avon dispatched its fall color story from its snazzy
midtown Manhattan offices up here to Suffern so the
swatches and swipe could be transubstantiated into lipsticks and eye shadows, a transition the industry calls
"sending it to the bench." (A "bench" is the lab; specif-
ically, it's the countertop where the chemist works.)
Since Avon has had a factory here for over a hundred
years, Suffern has color matching down to a routine.
First, they pin down the product development people:
Are the swatches and swipe supposed to show the color
in its packaging? Or after it's applied? Pan appeal or
payoff?

Once those issues are settled, the chemist heads for
the factory's Color Library, which keeps samples of
every makeup color produced by Avon during the last
decade: over five thousand colors, including about seventeen hundred lipsticks. The chemist finds a sample
that looks pretty close to the new one, finds its formula,

and uses that as a starting point. No sense reinventing the wheel.

For a product like lipstick, the basics have been boringly consistent for decades. Every lipstick boils down to pigment dispersed in a carrier. Usually that carrier is something like carnuba wax (the same stuff used on cars) to give the stick shape, plus enough oil to make it glide. From there, it gets trickier. Different pigments have different properties. Frosts make lipstick hard. The pigments known as "aluminum lakes" make lipstick mushy. Pearls have to be put in toward the end of the cooking or they disintegrate, like real pearls dropped in vinegar.

The labs themselves look like chem classrooms in a community college. Color labs face north, because that's the best light to match color. (Direct sun is too yellow.) Inside, men and women in lab coats carry little cups of colors back and forth, grind pigments, crank hand presses to create sample pans of eye shadows, and pour beakers of liquid lipstick into bullet-shaped molds. When it's time for product evaluation, there's a lot of swiping of lipsticks and eye shadows on the backs of hands, then squinting and staring at the swipes. The same as at company headquarters. The same as a shopper standing in a store.

Usually the first set of lab samples is ready within a couple of weeks, whereupon it's sent back to Manhattan as a submission. Invariably, it comes back. And goes again. And comes back again. And again. And again. Normally, it takes six rounds of submissions to get everything the way everyone wants it, although Suffern says it has suffered through as many as twenty rounds of rejection. This fall's story, a nice-enough looking bunch of colors that started out being called "Fresco" and is now known as "A Moment in Tuscany," took eight weeks to work out. About average.

Right now, "A Moment in Tuscany" is on the lipstick production line on the first floor of the factory, and the chemists and labs have already moved on to their next color story.

On Suffern's famous "lipstick line," very pleasant-looking ladies, heads covered by the kind of paper shower caps worn in operating rooms and industrial kitchens, peer intently at hundreds of uncapped lipsticks moving past them on a conveyor belt. In the big, garage-type space around the ladies, equally nice and similarly attired men and women attend to an assortment of Rube Goldberg contraptions. Like a set for an *I Love Lucy* episode, the big machines clink and clunk along.

Such is the stuff that dreams are made on.

A woman is attracted to lipstick by stories, promises, and possibilities. Why worry about what's in it? Isn't the FDA supposed to take care of that?

For centuries, people painted or powdered their faces with lead, which not only poisoned them, but pockmarked their skin in the process. At various points in those pre-FDA days, people put two and two together and decided that lead was a doubtful beauty aid. And then kept using it until something better came along.

History books brim with unhealthy cosmetic customs. Egyptians used antimony in eye makeup. Romans did it because the Egyptians did. Restoration beauties put belladonna in their eyes to dilate the pupils. Victorians ingested arsenic to improve complexions.

Most women, though, made cosmetics at home using innocuous ingredients in recipes passed along by friends or family. And most nice women didn't use cosmetics much. Outside court circles, the heavy users were prostitutes, actors, people at the margins of society.

That changed in the nineteenth century, when patent medicine makers branched into beauty. Cosmetics, like everything else that had been made at home, went industrial. No one could be sure what went into them.

In 1906, when Congress created the Pure Food and Drug Act, the progenitor of today's regulatory system, a few people wanted it to include cosmetics. But in 1906 the beauty industry was considered so inconsequential that its inclusion would have lowered the tone of the legislation. Also, the beauty industry affected only women. And women couldn't vote.

Even so, the 1906 act could have curbed the beauty business if anyone had been interested in applying it. The law banned lead and discouraged radium. Mislabeling could be prosecuted, especially if a beauty company had the hubris to claim its product changed any function of the body (which legally meant it was making a drug claim).

But men had more important things on their minds, so lead snuck into cosmetics and mislabeling ran rampant. During the 1920s, cosmetics manufacturers made shameless claims and converted millions of women to makeup. Not even the Depression slowed sales.

By the 1930s, the industry was getting away with murder. A fifty-two-year-old woman was fatally poisoned by Lash-Lure, a mascara substitute. Koremlu, a depilatory made with rat poison, crippled scores of women. Cuticle removers removed fingernails and fingertips along with cuticles. Acetone, carbolic acid, coaltar dyes, formaldehyde, and mercury were common ingredients. Dandruff remedies incorporated arsenic.

In 1933, the FDA put together its "Chamber of Horrors," an exhibit intended to pump up support for the Tugwell Bill, an amendment to the 1906 act that would have given the FDA jurisdiction over the beauty industry. Among other mutilations made in the name of beauty, the FDA showed graphic photos—complete with contorted eye sockets—of a woman who had been blinded by Lash-Lure. The shock tactics got publicity, but didn't get the bill passed. Lash-Lure wasn't even pulled off the market.

The beauty industry had lobbied aggressively against the bill, arguing that factory inspection would reveal trade secrets and ingredient names would only confuse women who, poor dears, were unfamiliar with big scientific words. A 1934 exposé, *Skin Deep* by M. C. Phillips, quotes the manager of a cosmetics company as saying, "Remove confidence from our business, and we might as well be selling pretty bottles and little boxes full of water and air."

Finally, in 1938, New Dealers pushed through passage of the Food, Drug, and Cosmetic Act, which gave the FDA authority to seize a mislabeled or injurious cosmetic after it had been sold in interstate commerce. For the first year, most of what they seized was Lash-Lure. When the manufacturer was brought to court, she pleaded no contest and got off with a $250 fine.

Next the feds went after a company that produced a copycat Lash-Lure. Those defendants got a suspended one-year sentence. The FDA cited Guerlain for selling lipsticks containing cadmium and selenium, which were considered poisonous. Guerlain shipped the lipsticks back to Paris and sold them there. Similar infractions incurred similar penalties.

When the U.S. entered World War II, the government ordered a 20 percent curtailment in cosmetics manufacture to conserve metal, mineral oil, and other components for the war effort. Four months later, thanks to vigorous battling by the beauty industry, the order was rescinded and rationing was made voluntary. The beauty industry then geared up for its own war effort by promoting lipstick as essential to U.S. morale and showing how leg makeup could substitute for nylon stockings. Sales increased again.

In 1960, federal law mandated labeling of hazardous substances. Cosmetics remained exempt. The same year, a law banning the use of certain dyes in foods was extended to include lipsticks. The law was conservative. The dyes were proven poisons. The beauty industry protested anyway. As Toni Stabile reported in her 1966 exposé, *Cosmetics: Trick or Treat?*, executives from Avon, Helena Rubinstein, and Revlon swore up and down that their own testing made federal intervention unnecessary.

Only a year or so after those outraged protestations, the same three companies (plus Max Factor, Maybelline, and at least a dozen lesser-known names) were caught using the offending ingredient in Lash-Lure. Hundreds of women across the country had reported severe allergic reactions to eye pencils that, as it turned out, had all been sourced from the same factory in Tennessee. The factory owner said—oops!—he had no idea the ingredient had been banned since 1938. He'd been using it for years with no complaints.

All that happened after the 1966 Fair Packaging and Labeling Act had supposedly mandated ingredient listing on cosmetic labels. Again, the law was conservative. Its main purpose was to help consumers identify allergens: fragrances, flavors, and "trade secrets" were exempt. But the beauty industry lobbied against it, so labeling wasn't fully implemented until 1976.

Not that the FDA's Office of Cosmetics has ever had

it easy. Its annual budget is only $3.2 million (about what a mid-sized brand spends on advertising), and its manpower is minuscule. Taxpayers, who tend to be more concerned about the safety of their foods and drugs than their lipsticks, don't put it high on the political agenda.

Mostly, the beauty industry likes things that way. Recently, the industry was confronted with the possibility that the FDA's Office of Cosmetics might be moved away from the Center for Foods, where it currently resides, to the Center for Drug Evaluation, where there are lots of doctors who like to look at clinical studies. Whereupon the industry lobbied Congress for an extra $2.5 million to keep the Office of Cosmetics right where it is.

That still doesn't put the industry and the feds in complete cahoots. Decades after a ban on known carcinogens, the beauty industry still hasn't finished fighting. (This is the same industry that, not so long ago, defended "Lethal Dosage 50," a test that involved feeding one hundred lab animals lipstick until fifty died.) The Delaney clause, as it's known, is currently interpreted to mean that any admitted cancer risk is unacceptable—no matter how infinitesimal. Through the Cosmetics, Toiletries and Fragrance Association, its big, Washington, D.C.–based trade association, the industry argues, in effect, that an infinitesimal risk of cancer is okay. When it comes to the clinch, the industry is always on the side of deregulation.

So battles rage on. Regulations come and go. Women wear lipstick regardless.

Many a beauty secret is there for the asking. Through the Freedom of Information Act, anyone can request a copy of a beauty factory's inspection report. (The FDA website prompts you through the process. After that, you pay a processing fee and wait a few weeks for the information to arrive.)

Alas, reports are rarely worth the wait. Punctiliously protecting anything the beauty business calls a trade secret, the reports can arrive so censored with black marker that they look like letters from the front in an old war movie.

They're not up-to-the-minute news either. The agency can only cover about one hundred inspections a year, so not every factory gets inspected every year. For example: A consumer complained that Maybelline's Ultra Thick Ultra Lash Mascara caused nausea, chills, and fever. The mascara had been made at Maybelline's million-square-foot factory in Little Rock, so the FDA and the Arkansas State Department of Health jointly followed up—although they didn't get around to doing it until three years after the complaint. That's when they discovered that the offending product had already been discontinued. The inspectors couldn't find anything wrong at the factory and recommended another inspection in five years. End of story.

Lots of inspections seem to be prompted by complaints from competitors: proof of how "self-regulating" the beauty industry can be. A rival sics the FDA on Lauder because they've spotted a labeling discrepancy on a Clinique product. Someone else tattles on Avon, because an expiration date was missing on a sun protection product.

Otherwise the FDA inspector would have to be psychic to uncover dark doings or dastardly deeds. He or she has no right to consumer complaints, formulas, or manufacturing records. (A system that gives the company a chance to settle product liability cases on its own, shushing consumer complaints before they attract unwelcome attention.) At the factory, an FDA inspector is allowed to take samples and look around, and not much more. The reports' entertainment value comes from reading between the lines to see how uncooperative a factory can be while staying within the letter of the law: like a manager forbidding an FDA inspector to use the factory photocopier. Read enough and you get the impression that beauty companies do not take kindly to regulation.

The industry's alternative safety check is something called the Cosmetic Ingredient Review. The CTFA, which administers the voluntary review, argues that no outside watchdog would be more vigilant. After all, who could be better motivated to keep a nice, safe status quo?

If makeup did any *real* harm, customers would die,

survivors would sue, women would stop buying, and profits would stop.

What you don't know, you can make up as you go along. Beauty is the business of self-creation.

Suzi Weiss-Fischman was helping her brother-in-law run the dental supply company he'd bought for $50,000, when it dawned on the two of them that nail products were made out of pretty much the same stuff as dentures. Odontorium Products Inc. was shortened to OPI. Now, fourteen years after entering the manicure business full-time, OPI's revenues are $50 million.

Susan Yee and her five sisters were makeup junkies who'd wasted money on the wrong colors too many times. In 1991, top brands were either very pink or very apricot and looked awful on Asian skin. Borrowing $50,000 from their parents and anteing up $50,000 of their own, they decided to do mail-order for the Asian market. In a couple of years, Zhen was breaking mail-order response records.

Anthony Gill and Cristina Bornstein were obscure husband-and-wife artists who created "chakra" nail polishes for a conceptual art installation. The show tanked, but someone told them they'd do better with beauty. A few beauty products tanked too (e.g., "Balance," an especially grotesque green nail polish), but their color therapy concept sounded great to the beauty editors. So it was onward and upward to aromatherapy lipsticks. Only a year after its start, Tony & Tina had nationwide distribution in department and specialty stores.

If you've already got a big company going, selling makeup is like a license to print money. If you don't? There are all sorts of ways to get around that.

"We had no product. No concept of product," says Stacey Schieffelin, remembering back, over two years ago now, when she started her company.

In those days, Stacey was eight months pregnant and unemployed for the first time in her life. Arcing her arms a foot or so in front of her stomach to conjure that two-hundred-pound self, she says, "I was sitting there thinking, 'What am I gonna do? I'm used to runnin'. I can't just sit at home.'"

Up until then, Stacey modeled. She was never one of those superstar, instant-recognition faces. But she was tall and blond and as all-American-looking as you could get. And she worked like a dog. For two decades, she booked through fifteen different agencies around the world, averaged three hundred days a year, and racked up fifty-two countries on her passport.

Now here she was, in no shape to travel, with a new husband and her first baby on the way. She'd studied fashion merchandising, architecture, and broadcast journalism—and always fallen back on modeling.

At this point in her story, Stacey's voice goes slow and

low, like someone building suspense for a tale told many, many times before. "My husband was trying to calm me down," she recalls, "and he asked me, 'What do models prefer to do when they get out of the industry?'"

Those were the magic words. "What do models prefer?" Bells rang. Fireworks went off. "All those years of modeling . . . I'd spent years putting on makeup!" thought Stacey, and she decided right then and there to go into the beauty business.

She knew nothing about cosmetic chemistry. Her business background was nonexistent. Her financing was zilch. But, displaying a disregard for reality easily the equal of Madame or Miss Arden or Estée, Stacey went ahead and wangled a meeting at Home Shopping Network.

Her pitch was that she'd have the first beauty company created by a model. (Which wasn't *strictly* true: Other models, like the Danielson sisters who created BeneFit Cosmetics, developed their own brands. Still, it was *essentially* true: Most models fronted lines developed by somebody else.) Stacey called this nonexistent company "Models Prefer."

HSN went for it. They scheduled her for an eight-minute slot. She now had sixteen weeks to scramble for something to sell.

"It's balls to the walls time!" an exec at HSN told her. So Stacey anted up her ICMAD dues and sallied forth to trade shows, where she hit one brick wall after another. Nobody wanted to do business with her. Most weren't even polite about it. Small suppliers were cliquish. Big suppliers were more gracious, but just as unhelpful because their production schedules couldn't be interrupted for the kind of small order she needed. No thanks at all to hoity-toity trade show types, Stacey finally found small suppliers willing to take credit cards. Because, on top of having no product and no supply network, she also had no business plan, no investors, and no money. "David and I had been through divorces, so we were both broke."

She went on the air with one product: a liquid lip liner. She sold out in two minutes. HSN gave her three more shows. All of them went like gangbusters. Stacey then wangled a meeting with QVC, the shopping channel with the biggest audience. She stocked ten thousand lip liners for her first eight-minute appearance; they were gone in four.

QVC wanted more. Stacey stalled until she could invent something. By June 20, less than a year and a half after she'd come up with the idea for her company, she was backstage at QVC, getting ready to do an hour of live TV. Suddenly someone ran into the green room. The segment ahead of her had finished early. She had to go on. Right away.

"I said, 'David! What am I gonna do? Hair in rollers? No makeup?'" Stacey remembers, getting breathless just from retelling this part. Her husband told her to just go on anyway. At least she wouldn't intimidate anyone.

No one warned the host, who greeted her with

"Stacey! Evidently you don't know we're on the air!" She improvised again, demonstrating on live TV just how dramatically cosmetics could change a woman. Everything sold out in forty-two minutes.

That was last summer. According to her QVC contract, she had to sell $1.5 million that first year. She sold $7 million. That should double this year. She's not on the air all the time, which doesn't matter because she racks up $1 million days when she is. Shipments for a single show fill nine fifty-three-foot tractor-trailers.

Stacey has stuck with the hair-in-rollers schtick. Those ladies lingering over the makeup counters back in the mall are the same ones tuning in to her. As Stacey says: "My core customer, she's a soccer mom," and that soccer mom loves the on-air transformation. And QVC loves Stacey because each show lands the network three or four hundred customers who've never ordered from television before.

All the trendy companies—Hard Candy, SmashBox, Philosophy, Tony & Tina—are now on shopping channels too. Stacey, who talks as fast and fervently as a televangelist even when she's not on TV, says: "They can do more volume in that one hour than they probably can do in the store in six months."

Business is too good for her to bear any grudges. Her big, handsome, Harvard-educated husband works for her now. She has her own network of about thirty suppliers, which includes Intercos, the prestigious European firm that supplies the likes of Estée Lauder. Her lipsticks cost as much as Lancôme's. Her lipstick cases are made in the same mold as Guerlain's. Her product runs are so big—sixty-five to seventy-five thousand—that the factories who snubbed her a year or two ago wouldn't be able to handle her volume now.

Cosmetics can change lives. Stacey proves it every time she goes on the air.

January

PACKAGING: ALL WRAPPED UP

ONE BY ONE, town cars and taxis pull up to 60 East 65th Street and discharge pale, bare-legged women who do a high-heeled sprint into Restaurant Daniel.

This is one of those midwinter, midweek gray days, when Manhattan clicks along, relentless as a stock ticker. Neither a postholiday lull nor rumor of recession has slowed the moneyed bustle of midtown. The ladies heading into the restaurant, the elect of the beauty press, wear the harried look of women who have too many appointments like this, too many lunches and launches and champagne celebrations to attend.

Late January is high season for introductions. Packaging and proprietary ingredients and spokesmodel signings and other commendable but excruciatingly unsexy announcements are made at the rate of one or two a day, a semiannual orgy of self-congratulation that won't end until runway shows start—which means no respite for a couple of weeks.

Today's luncheon heralds yet another launch. This afternoon, Neutrogena unveils new packaging, new makeup, and new advertising. Following the unwritten protocol of the industry, a company sold in drugstores and discount outlets has chosen a very exclusive, extremely expensive setting to woo women who rarely wear makeup and wouldn't be caught dead shopping for it in Wal-Mart if they did. Haute cuisine from Daniel Bouloud, Manhattan's chef of the moment, will be served. Champagne toasts will be made. Commissioned gifts will be given.

As is expected. According to those same unwritten rules, the more mass the product, the more class its presentation. In the beauty industry, some of the best stories are told by the curve of a compact's corners, the color of its cardboard box, and the menu of luncheons like this one.

The characters assemble inside the restaurant's anteroom. In contrast to the press, the Neutrogena people all look pleased as punch to be here. Happiness shines out of their faces. Some of them have been waiting two years for this. They do their best to mix, talking animatedly and using lots of phrases like "Neutrogena equity."

The beauty editors sip their flutes of flat water and do their best to look fascinated. They nod as though they've never heard this story before. None carries a notebook.

"It's really a skin care line that just happens to be color cosmetics too," explains an upbeat executive in what passes for cocktail chitchat at these events. The editor standing opposite him lets her eye drift to the silvery salver of hors d'oeuvres passing on her left. Risotto balls with white truffle. She flaps her wrist at the tray and turns her attention back to the executive. "We're growing the equity," he continues.

A woman whose card reads "Lip, Eye, and New Categories" explains that brand-new packaging debuts today. She looks ebullient. No way this one could go wrong. Not with all the prep work that went into it. Not with $20 million in advertising budgeted to back it up. No way.

Like the other executives here this afternoon, Miss Lip, Eye, and New Categories has been flown in from company headquarters in California for this. She's been with the company for a year and a half, the last six months of it working on this line. Before that, she worked for Clairol, although apparently beauty has been a lifelong obsession: "My mother will tell you I was never without a lipstick and a hairbrush."

Miss Lip talks and talks about the new line. The editor opposite her just needs to stand still and smile. "We slightly overcompensated on the beautiful," Miss Lip faux-bashfully admits. "Then, we tracked consumer behavior trends. Are women spending more or less time on the face?" She never gets around to answering that one, because a beaming Yohini Appa comes up to greet her and gladhand the editors.

Yohini, who directs the company's research and development, looks about to burst with enthusiasm over the new products and packaging. She also looks like a walking, talking product endorsement. Aside from today's outfit, which is an exact match to the company cartons right down to the stripes in her blouse, Yohini has absurdly abundant hair and a poured-caramel complexion that either God or Neutrogena created without visible pores. Even more impressive, she has a Ph.D. in organic chemistry coupled with sufficient social poise to explain her job to members of the beauty press who did not do notably well in their science studies during college.

Her cocktail chatter is full of factoids about skin and hair. Let other executives fret about trends and textures and such subjective concerns. For Yohini, beauty is reassuringly quantifiable. There is, for instance, an ideal temperature for skin. "At twenty-eight degrees centigrade you get nonapparent sweating. Your stratum corneum is more hydrated. Another bit of trivia!" she cheerily offers. There's also an ideal humidity. "That's 80 to 85 percent—but then you're not comfortable."

"One must suffer to be beautiful!" says an editor. The little group chuckles appreciatively at her aperçu.

"I was in Fiji," Miss Lip chimes in. "It rained twice a day. Everyone had *beautiful* skin."

A salver of pumpkin barbajuan passes. Waiters proffer water and champagne, water proving the more popular beverage. (Beauty editors are an abstemious lot, constantly thinking of appearances.) A flash pops periodically, as the photographer from *Women's Wear Daily* records the assembly. The Neutrogena executives proudly wear makeup from their line. The editors don't seem to wear any makeup at all. The sunny Californians talk of "consumer behavior trends" and "market research groups" and "focus groups." The New Yorkers, uniformed in black and gray as if it's a secret dress code, listen without a lot of comment.

A company like this comes to cosmetics with a different mind-set than an entrepreneur without a huge operation already in place and a bottom line carefully watched by lots of accountants who like their jobs. It tries to research, even when research may not really apply. It does homework. It assiduously tests products, whenever possible, on what it refers to as "real women." Meaning women who live outside New York and L.A. in the land where makeup comes from malls and Wal-Marts. Meaning women who aren't dressed in gray yet and don't sport high heels with bare legs in the middle of winter.

When it owned Elizabeth Arden, Chesebrough-

Ponds used to try out new products in Minot, North Dakota (Town motto: "Why not Minot?"), a site well-supplied with the two essentials of cosmetics testing: rotten weather and willing subjects. In Minot, the average snowfall is twenty-six inches, the average winter high is fifteen degrees fahrenheit, the average low goes way below zero, and gusts off the Great Plains can whip up quite a windburn.

Playing guinea pig was nice, easy money for the real women of Minot, a place haloed by buried missile silos and mile after mile of not much else. The women used to make anywhere from $35 to $100 for up to two weeks of participation, and most test protocols involved nothing more than a few minutes of filling out a questionnaire and being looked at by a technician. The worst part about the whole thing, one woman remembers, was having to leave the house in the morning without her own makeup on.

Yohini prefers Winnipeg, especially for testing dry skin products. She does her hot weather testing in Tucson. "But even there you might get a week of rain sometimes," she says sadly. When all else fails, she resorts to her own climate-controlled room at Neutrogena. "But I chart the weather patterns," she adds brightly, "I'm always calling LAX and asking them about storms."

Today's makeup was tested in Colorado Springs and Dallas, where panels of eighty to one hundred real women were recruited on the theory that, if you recruit a big enough group, you get the distribution of skin types—oily, dry, sensitive, whatever—that's in the general population.

Lipsticks were tested for conditions like "cupping," one of Yohini's many bits of skin trivia. "Lip skin has a vermilion border between the moist, mucousy membrane and the dry skin on the lip," explains Yohini, sounding like she lives for this sort of thing. "Right at that border you'll get little crescent shapes if your lips are dry—that's cupping." The technicians just kept measuring until they found a formula that made cupping go away.

Like any conscientious clinician, Yohini does her best to keep variables to a minimum. In her ideal world, lousy weather would last three months at a stretch, thus guaranteeing that any measurable improvement was not the result of a refreshing rainstorm or bout of balmy temperatures. On a real woman, a beauty product's true value becomes apparent when there's not much else going on.

Few of makeup's pleasures are palpable. And, of those, its physical packaging is the most dependable. The only effect that never varies with lighting or comes loaded with issues of self-esteem or disappoints once you leave the store.

Confronted with new makeup, there is always that first moment when the reluctance to ravish wars with the impulse to experience. If she's bought from a department store or direct sales, a woman pries open a pretty box. If she's bought from a drugstore, she lifts protective plastic molded over the makeup like the shield guarding the charmed slumber of Snow White.

Inside is her own small and perfect object. Her own lipstick. She can now roll its carefully calibrated heft in the palm of her hand, unclick its cap, see that unsullied stick of color swivel obediently toward her. Make the automatic swipe across the back of her hand. Or rush the unspoiled, softly slanted tip right to her lips. Study its effect. Consider. Reapply. Watch the stick retreat at the touch of a finger. Hear that cunningly crafted cap click into place like the miniature echo of a limousine door *thwump*ing shut.

Each layer of packaging is another assurance that this lipstick is hers alone. It has not been tried on and rejected. It has not been worn and contaminated. The makeup comes to her pure, pristine, perfectly hygenic. No matter how many other women wear the same shade or buy the same brand, this one is all hers.

A beauty product becomes impossible to sell in a crumpled box or a dented shield. Damaged containers equal damaged goods, even when the makeup itself remains inviolate. Otherwise eco-conscious women resist attempts to eliminate the extra tissue or cardboard.

Women don't seem much interested in buying a stick of colored wax and inserting it into their old lipstick case. Well-meaning companies who conscientiously offer reusable metal containers soon discover that most customers still buy a brand-new one every time. Makeup artists' palettes, designed to corral colors into utilitarian uniformity, are rarely used by anybody but makeup artists. Forgoing the pleasure of so much shiny newness is too high a price to pay for saving a few dollars.

Knowing that, the CTFA, the industry's powerful trade association, has lobbied against state-level initiatives that would restrict beauty packaging. (Only direct sales companies, whose catalog businesses are least contingent on the charms of wrappers and boxes, have made any headway in reducing excess.)

Packaging turns all the vague promises of beauty into something substantial. Open your purse and the lipstick is right there, something you've picked from among thousands of possibilities, something lovely in and of itself. Like beautiful binding on a favorite book, something tangibly lovely wrapped around the intangibly lovely story inside.

For the first few thousand years, cosmetics' packaging didn't matter so much. People put color on their faces to fend off evil spirits or engage in rituals or look more attractive to the opposite sex. Most people improvised their own. Then, as the Western world industrialized, custom created industry. Supply outgrew demand. By the late 1800s, there was enough makeup around for women to wonder why to buy one brand instead of the next. Packaging provided an answer.

The stuff inside always seemed to be the same. Rouge was red. So was lipstick. Powder was white, pink, or brown. Mascara was black. In the days before color stories, there was no reason for a woman to buy more until the original was used up. Then early entrepreneurs figured out that, if the packaging was pretty enough, women would consider makeup a collectible instead of a commodity.

France led the fashion. Finding they could charge more for face powders that came in eye-catching cartons, companies like Coty commissioned containers from designers like Leon Bakst, an artist who did décors and costumes for Diaghilev's Ballets Russes. (Coty's current bestseller is a design from 1914, which the company enjoys attributing to René Lalique.) At around the same time, Bourjois got the brainstorm of putting eye shadow in pretty flowered boxes, turning a cosmetic identified with chorus girls and call girls into a dressing table staple of the bourgeoisie.

The signal event came in 1915, when American Maurice Levy invented the modern lipstick case. Lip color in stick form had been around as long ago as ancient Ur, but no one had thought to put it in a sturdy little container that swiveled like a toy and shone like jewelry.

For the next fifteen or twenty years, lip color and formula didn't change much, but the cases it came in did. A woman could buy ingenious pop-ups designed to be used with one hand. Or she could wield an elegant case covered with all manner of elaborate engravings and embellishments. She could buy jeweled gold or platinum cases at Cartier. Or she could buy the cases that Helena Rubinstein copied from Cartier.

Meanwhile, compacts rose to a rank somewhere between stockings and gloves on a woman's list of necessary niceties. They were made in cute shapes like books and guitars and flowers. They were travel souvenirs. People collected them. Jewelers produced them in precious metals and enamels. Women flourished them to display wit or wealth.

In the kind of chicken-or-egg conundrum that keeps social anthropologists in business, no one can figure out if the pretty packaging or the public application came first. But by the 1930s, it was impossible to imagine one without the other. Women developed an entire vocabulary of gestures related to makeup, while etiquette books mooted the fine points of flaunting lipsticks and compacts in mixed company.

Distinctions evolved. Elizabeth Arden's fetish for pink packaging obliged rivals to avoid it. Soon each company had a signature shade. French packaging remained fanciful. Americans approached it with greater gravitas. Mass-market packaging had to be cheap, easy to ship, and show enough of the color to lure an impulse shopper. Direct sales packaging, like Avon's and Mary Kay's, didn't have to be very good at all, since it didn't have to lure anybody anywhere.

Packaging was used to tell all kinds of stories. The 1960s exaltation of youth and innocence—not qualities traditionally associated with cosmetics—brought packaging that was playful and purposely inelegant. Lip color came in little pots that were a sticky-fingered mess to use, and as different as could be from mom's old-fashioned swivel stick of Max Factor. Eye shadows came in children's paint sets. In the 1970s Clinique launched with hospital green and chrome containers that looked sterile and surgically minimal next to the lah-di-dah blue and gold curlicues of Estée Lauder, its parent company.

Embossing, a fleeting pleasure at best, was applied directly to lipstick tips and pans of powder. Couldn't afford thousands for a quilted Chanel bag? Then buy a Chanel eye shadow stamped with the same quilting. The effect was ruined the first time you used the product; but that only added to the throwaway elegance of it all.

In the 1990s, magnetized compacts supposedly symbolized consumer empowerment because a consumer could swap around the eye shadows and blushers whenever she wanted, instead of being stuck with some marketer's selection. Cheap plastic, the generic stuff used by jobbers, symbolized the rebel: packaging to show that packaging didn't count.

Buy a lipstick, get an image and philosophy and identity thrown in for free.

"Packaging implies the nature of the product inside. It's how the customer perceives herself," says designer

Marc Rosen, who teaches such things at the Pratt Institute and who, during his twenty-five years in the business, has also designed complete cosmetic lines for Chloé, Oscar de la Renta, Fendi, and Karl Lagerfeld.

If makeup by Chloé, Oscar de la Renta, Fendi, and Karl Lagerfeld doesn't ring any bells, that's because none ever got made. "The tooling would have cost too much," Rosen says wistfully. "Creating packaging is a huge financial commitment."

Changing packaging is no picnic either. Retooling costs a pile of money. Getting extant stock off store shelves costs another one. "You're talking about at least a million dollars," says Rosen. So when a company wants to update its image, it usually changes cartons and labels instead. Graphics get tweaked. Lancôme's logo rose grows larger, then smaller, then larger again. Estée Lauder's swirly monogram goes from rococo to neoclassic to romantic.

Cost is why undercapitalized startup lines use stock packaging—the basic black, no-frills factory stuff that can be stamped with anybody's name. "Companies buy stock and then pay people like me to tart it up," says Rosen. "There are all kinds of tricks. Like you can put weight on the bottom of a lipstick, so it feels heavier and more expensive."

Of course, even stock packaging has a subtext: Not fussing with the container implies that the stuff inside is more important. That works well enough for makeup artists starting their own lines. Although it's not something a big brand or a high-end line can get away with. "Packaging is really about a persona," says Rosen. "If you're trying to convey a certain image in this market, you absolutely must get the packaging right. Otherwise, you might as well not launch at all."

Pity the package designer.

Package design is part of the subliminal sell of cosmetics. As much or more than the rest of the industry, it is a completely arbitrary world. All decisions are based on opinion. Nothing is quantifiable. Nitpicky details have earth-shattering import. Frustrated that they can't measure taste and emotion the same way they measure skin moisture or sun protection, companies try anyway. And try. And try.

Nothing is too inconsequential to escape deliberation and fuss and testing on a focus group. The weight of cardboard, the heft of a bottle, the beveling of an edge are supposed to speak volumes to the consumer. And the presence or absence of those design details can easily add hundreds of thousands of dollars to the cost of manufacturing. Thus spelling bottom line–defined success. Or failure.

"Literally hundreds of designs left our tables here," says Mark Yoshimoto, with the wrung-out smile of a man who's made it through the marathon without a single shortcut. Mark has been with Neutrogena seventeen years; a lot of the last two were spent on the packaging premiering today.

When it started, the project was prosaic enough: conscientiously shopping all the trade shows and suppliers to see who had what in the United States, France, Japan, and Indonesia. Comparing components, turnaround times, costs, and assorted lipstick logistics.

Then came the semiotic stuff. Like corporate identity. Mark can natter on for a good five minutes about the "squarish with a bevel" appearance of the company's liquid soap being echoed by the shape of the new compacts. With passionate pedantry, he explains that "the edges aren't so square and hard, they're slightly rounded—to go with the Neutrogena equity." Like a screenwriter assigned to add a sexy storyline to a Disney production, Mark had to resolve all the earnest, therapeutic associations of the brand with makeup, a category that innately speaks of artifice and illusion.

Package designers draw inspiration from different places than the people in product development. It doesn't help them to fly to Première Vision and look at the fabrics that will be fashionable next year. Like their colleagues in the car industry, they look at the longer range. Detroit is their Paris. "We definitely avoid color forecasts," says Mark. "We avoid anything trendy."

When Mark's team came up with a promising design, it was tested on consumer focus groups. Those focus groups liked a couple of the early attempts, because everything looked like they expected. That was bad. "You have to see through their comments," Mark says wearily. Would women want to pull the compact out of their purse and flash it around at a restaurant?

Well, no. It's something I would use if my skin had problems.

Back to the drawing board.

Color was probably the toughest call. As it always has been. When Estée Lauder was looking for her signature shade, she decided that the color had to look good in bathrooms. So she loaded her purse with colored samples and, anytime she went out, would head for the nearest bathroom to see how they looked. That, so she said, is how she arrived at "Estée Lauder blue," a pale turquoise. But then Estée operated in the days before focus groups.

Neutrogena tested black. Focus groups liked black. Lots of makeup artists' lines use black. Testing showed that black was, in design-speak, "a good Neutrogena color cue." Except that the products would be going into stores right beside walls of Revlon products packaged in black.

Back to the drawing board.

White was a good color. White was clean. White fit the Neutrogena image. But white plastic can look cheesy. It gets dirty. It stains.

Back to the drawing board.

Blue was another Neutrogena color. Blue is accepting. Blue is credible. Blue is America's favorite color. But blue tested with a fifty-fifty split: 50 percent of the focus groups *loved* the blue. Which means that the other 50 percent did not.

Back to the drawing board.

Burgundy belonged to Maybelline. Gray belonged to L'Oréal.

Forget orange. Forget green. Both too polarizing. As Mark puts it: "You want a color where no one will say, 'Eech! That is absolutely ugly.'"

Metallic was showing up on a lot of those long-range forecasts so beloved by car companies and the makers of major appliances. Metallic has always been popular for sound equipment. Metallic packaging isn't seen much in drugstores, since it's more expensive to produce than plastic. Plus—here's the clincher—metallic tested as non-polarizing.

Metallic it was.

But not just any metallic. Mark's department wanted a warm one.

Bronze, copper, and gold were out. They'd been around for eons. So the designers tried a not-quite-gold and not-quite-bronze with a smidgen of not-quite-pewter. They matted the finish, to make it less flashy, "more Neutrogena," then trademarked it with the name "Char-gold."

Basically, it's beige.

Mark seems not the least perturbed that the roads are gridlocked with Acura Integras and Toyota Camrys that have rounded corners and warm metallics and matte finishes. "I just bought a hairdryer that color," he volunteers, with the serenity of a man totally in tune with the zeitgeist.

Everywhere a woman turns, she's going to see some

useful object that reminds her of Neutrogena. No company could ask for a better subliminal sell.

Like most of what goes on in a cosmetics factory, packaging tests aren't state-of-the-art science, but they do the trick. First, someone has to make sure contents and containers are compatible: High oil content breaks down certain plastics. High alcohol content destroys styrene and PVC.

Once that's resolved, environment has to be factored in. Makeup gets steamed in humidity chambers to approximate a day in New Orleans. Baked in ovens to approximate a day in Phoenix. Cooled in refrigerators to approximate a winter in Boston. Eventually, the company comes up with something that doesn't melt or crack. After that, they try to make it fall apart.

There is, for instance, the scuff test, which Neutrogena's packaging director describes as: "Taking two compacts and rubbin' 'em together real hard." And the kick test, which is just what it sounds like.

Then there's the jiggle test: Pack the makeup in cartons and put them on a vibration table for an hour to imitate conditions on the back of a truck.

The rub test: Put the packages in a vise next to some plastic and time how long it takes for the finish to wear off.

The drop test: Hold the packages at waist height and drop them. Then drop them again on different flooring.

(Continue bombardment until the packages have been dropped on all standard floorings.)

The purse test: Get handbags of different sizes and load them with purse paraphernalia like coins, paper clips, and cosmetics. Then tumble-dry for twenty minutes. (The purses are demolished, but a good lipstick or compact is supposed to make it out okay.)

If only it were all so easy.

Same look. Same color. Same timing. Whole different story.

Across town, another company is launching new makeup in new packaging, and it looks just like Neutrogena's.

Apparently, they have the same motive for doing it too. Lancaster, a high-priced beauty company based in Monaco and much more famous in Europe, is known here for skin care. The company hoped that adding makeup would be a way of selling more products without cannibalizing any of its existing business.

"We know color gets the consumer to the counter," says an exec. "We were losing customers. You hook 'em with treatment and they're going everywhere else for color."

So after issuing the usual boilerplate about capitalizing on its Monegasque heritage, Lancaster commissioned cosmetic formulas from a lab in Morris Plains, New Jersey. Then it assigned the project to Storm Design, a New York packaging specialist with Sears, Disney, and Ban deodorant on its résumé.

As design companies must, Storm dutifully produced storyboards for each concept it showed the client. (This one was "Radiant Beauty," a concept that supposedly speaks to the "sun and air and beauty" of life along the Mediterranean coast.) From there, the project went through eight more months of the kind of brainstorming and refining and beveling of edges that Mark and his team endured. Plus the inevitable testing on focus groups. They ended up with rounded corners and a beige metallic. William Crane, the president of Storm Design, who can be just as passionately pedantic about packaging design as Mark, says the containers allude to "European heritage" and Japanese worry stones.

At one point last year, Storm Design was working on three cosmetics projects at once, an experience that gave Crane a certain insight into the mojo of the makeup business. "Beauty companies aren't making their margins in fragrance anymore," he says. "And color has always been a very good business.

"It's not a huge capital expense to change a color palette," he points out. Get your packaging in place, plug in new pigments every season, and sit back and reap the profits. It costs next to nothing to switch one pigment for another. "With color cosmetics, you always have a brand-new product to sell. Without doing a launch. Without paying for new packaging."

Getting it going is the tough part.

. . .

Flickering candles illuminate the restaurant's private dining room as the press enters for its lunch. Inside, no stone has been left unturned, no expense forgone, no effort spared—exertions all the more gallant in light of the fact that few magazine editors are in any position to ignore a launch with $20 million of Johnson & Johnson advertising behind it.

In lieu of paintings, the room is decorated with framed photos of makeup. In lieu of place cards, editors' names are printed on makeup cartons. In lieu of conventional napkin rings, starched napkins are surmounted by lipstick tubes. Tablecloths match products. Centerpieces are—what else?—arty arrangements of packaging. And, lest all the drugstore display look a tad tawdry in these surroundings, each centerpiece is smothered in profligately pricey profusions of white, ivory, and parchment roses, stalks of full-blown lilies, and poetically trailing tendrils of ivy.

While lighting in the windowless room remains dramatically dim, the ladies of the beauty press are allowed a few minutes to nibble salad with black truffle dressing, then treated to a video reprising the company's greatest hits. For the first of what will be dozens and dozens of times during the next hour, the assembled gathering hears the buzzwords "beautiful and beneficial." The ladies clap politely.

Speeches are made: The first speaker manages to say

"beautiful" and "beneficial" several more times. Then the lights come up and waiters distribute the main course, fish with more black truffles.

The room holds eight tables each seating nine or ten people, with company executives scattered liberally throughout. Corporate honchos sit with big-shot editors from *Vogue*, *Elle*, and *Harper's Bazaar*. While the community liaison gets stuck with a freelancer and editors from *Fitness* and *Parents*. Executives respectfully refer to the women who pen prose on party hairdos and zit zapping as "journalists." The journalists remain courteously aloof, allowing themselves to be coaxed and courted.

Table talk inevitably turns to beauty products. Editors discuss, not particularly knowledgeably, cosmetic ingredients like coenzyme Q_{10}. "Now what's that supposed to do again? I always forget," asks one.

Her table companion doesn't know either. "But I don't think it's in any of our stuff."

When most people are done picking at their main course, the CEO makes a brief speech. Another speaker, working the words "beautiful" and "beneficial" into her talk more times than anyone would have guessed possible, praises the packaging. Much ado is made about Char-gold. As the highest of compliments, no editor pretends a pressing engagement to escape the presentation.

A toast is proposed to the new year, new products, new projects. Not everyone has champagne yet. In the spirit of the thing, they hold high their empty flutes and smile.

At long last, it's time for the fun stuff: gifts and goodies. Cozy little chocolate cakes appear at each place setting along with—as a sort of dessert to the dessert—one of the new powder boxes tied up with a pretty bow. Untying the bow, the editors find the company has commissioned a silver pendant for each of them. Its matte finish and rounded corners are meant to remind them of the new packaging.

No one rushes to put hers on.

This was supposed to be over by two and it's 2:30. Enough is enough. No one waits around for petits fours or coffee. Editors charge the coat check.

As a herd of women in high-heeled mules click-clack toward waiting town cars, public relations minions pass out more loot. Today's goody bags are special commissions too. In lieu of the standard shopping bag stuffed with products, the company has copied a Kate Spade tote (very popular with the magazine crowd when they are not toting Prada). Naturally, the tote is Char-gold, and someone has commissioned little "Neutrogena Cosmetics" labels and sewn them into the linings.

Inside are the usual color charts and press releases. Plus a few products, which seem like an afterthought. Today's story has been told.

. . .

February

THE RUNWAYS: TELLERS OF TALES

A FEW BLOCKS east of Times Square, the tents have taken over Bryant Park again.

Bent over by the bitter February cold, the itinerant workers of the fashion world drag their totes and wheelie suitcases through the encampment, past shivering, sleepy-looking guards sipping cardboard cups of scalding coffee. By mid-morning, the park will be under siege, surrounded by buyers, media, and gate-crashing groupies. All insisting on immediate entrée to shows that will already be running late.

At this bleak hour, there is zero excitement in the air and no eye candy in sight. For the jet-lagged models and makeup artists hurrying to their first call, the shows are just another job that starts another season's rotation of fashion capitals.

Not a single one of them has consulted a trend forecaster to find out what to do for fall. No one knows or cares about "Winter Beach" or any of the other color stories that have been so painstakingly produced over the preceding year. No one has the slightest interest in Neutrogena's new packaging. And if it occurred to anyone here that pink lipstick attracts soccer moms to Nordstrom counters, that would be reason enough not to use it. Nomads with complete disregard for the customs of the country, they are here to dazzle the populace and sow dissatisfaction with the status quo. And then move on.

This week, with tools gathered from the ends of the globe and techniques unpracticed by any outside their tribe, they will perform their customary feats of conjuring. Makeup will spin story lines for clothes that have none and embroider gorgeous fantasies across all those yards of unrelieved gray and snow-blinding winter white. Afterward, as they migrate onward to London and Milan and Paris, these stories will be retold in magazines, broadcast on television, reinterpreted at beauty counters, and endlessly quoted, translated, and plagiarized until the next runway season comes along.

What goes on here has nothing to do with marketing strategies or focus groups or anything else the beauty industry plots and plans. Runway shows are rife with challenges unimagined by ordinary mortals, flashes of wizardry, demonstrations of magic, and heroes and heroines larger than life.

All the makings of the most irresistible stories.

• • •

Backstage in the biggest tent, it's the standard set-up: Bad buffet in front, port-a-potty in the rear, hair and makeup tables forming one long gauntlet in between. Lights that make everyone look haggard and hideous. Photographers slung with kilos of cameras and flash units. Techies worrying into walkie-talkies.

First big show on the first morning of the season, so the gang's all here. Designer Carolina Hererra apportions elegantly abbreviated sound bites to a video crew. Dressers obsessively check and recheck stashes of lint rollers, insoles, and Static Guard. Small foreign women drift up and down the aisle grabbing hands to apply translucent nail polish that no one will notice from the runway. Three models share a cigarette and one-up each other with the awfulness of Milan: "I had a fish dress!" whines one. "Well, I had a fish coat!" says the second, dragging on the Marlboro Light. "I had a huge lobster from here to here," says the third, smugly trumping her friends, "Oh my God, was it *hideous!*"

Gisele Bündchen, the Brazilian model who will be the star of these shows—something somehow predestined weeks ago—gambols in, smacking and smooching all who stand in her way. Gisele, who has the personality of a bichon in the body of a borzoi, goofs her way down the gauntlet, then half spins and full halts with maximum melodrama. All five feet eleven inches and one hundred and ten pounds of her crumples into a makeup chair. Her smiley face collapses into a cartoon of misery. Gisele has a cold! Normally the happiest of creatures, Gisele dabs at her nose and sniffs pathetically. Where nobody can miss it.

Chilled to the bone, British makeup artist Linda Cantello arrives on the dot of 8 o'clock. Forty-plus, Linda shows the wilful lack of chic and conspicuously bare face that distinguish her as authentic backstage *noblesse*. Today she's in black pants, a sweater that looks like it came from her husband's closet, and crepe-soled Clarks Wallabees, an outfit she will adopt with minor variations for the rest of the week. Leaving her assistant to unpack, she heads off to hunt for coffee.

The assistant dusts off the stretch of pockmarked plywood allotted as Linda's makeup table, and unzips two totes and a suitcase packed to bursting with arcane brands. Alcone. Ben Nye. Inoui. Maquillage Paris/Berlin Professional. Ruby & Millie. Visiora. Judging by Linda's luggage, art and commerce don't overlap a lot.

Package designers would weep at the sight of this. Powders pried from compacts and pasted on trays. Lipsticks dug out of tubes and smeared into palettes. Hundreds and hundreds of products ignominiously sorted into unlabeled Baggies. Heinous shades like cobalt blue and kelly green and orange. All arrayed in front of a makeup mirror jury-rigged out of a dime-store mirror turned sideways and clamped with a couple of clip lights.

Linda reappears. Taking one last swig of caffeine from her styrofoam cup, she rounds up her crew. This morning's story appears to be an update of *La Côte*

Basque. In about an hour, these girls will glide down the runway like the swans of Truman Capote's roman à clef. Makeup and hair will be modeled on Carolina Herrera's own, which means everyone gets the sixty-year-old socialite's powdery skin, sleekly pouffed hair, and rich-lady red lipstick.

Starting the first girl, Linda sticks her fingers into a palette of greasepaints and mixes the shade she wants on the back of her hand. She pats the result on the model's cheeks where blusher would normally go. Then she powders a bit. She reaches into a Baggie and pulls out M·A·C's "Russian Red," a lipstick last fashionable about five years ago. Then she lets the model do her own mascara. That's it. The first big story of the season is finished.

The rest of the eighty-plus shows this week will follow pretty much the same format: Chaotic conditions, rotten lighting, and an ad hoc assortment of products that includes none of the foundation, lip liner, or other stuff that the beauty industry tells women to buy. Circumstances that could never be duplicated. Models who in no way approach the norm. Show after show of impossible glamour.

Runways work strong magic. Without it, many a makeup product is tenderly conceived, midwifed into the world with the greatest of care, and yet languishes unloved on store shelves—a Sleeping Beauty with no Prince Charming to confer his consummating kiss.

Back in the mid 1990s, black nail polish was being worn by Goths and club kids, subcultures of unimpeachable edginess. Dominique Szabo remembers noticing it on design students during one of her scouting trips to Première Vision. Having been in the business long enough to know a nascent trend when she saw one, Dominique decided to do a color story for Estée Lauder that included black nail polish. Remembering, Dominique's face takes on the expression Cassandra's must have had when the Greeks emerged from the Trojan horse to sack the city. As she wistfully recalls: "That was innovative. That was different." That also didn't sell.

At around the same time, a makeup artist at Chanel used black marker on the models' nails for some preshow publicity photos. When it came time for the actual show, she mixed a batch of almost-black polish and put it on all forty-five models. Since this was taking place at the scorching point of runway red-hotness, backstage was crawling with photographers and beauty editors looking for a story to report. Rich girls in screw-you Goth nail polish gave it to them.

Playing to the publicity windfall, Chanel swiftly added Vamp, an almost-black nail polish, to its line. Vamp wasn't radically unlike the Lauder polish, except in provenance. Everyone wanted the Chanel version of the story, including Madonna. Uma Thurman wore it in *Pulp Fiction*, the hipster hit of the year. *InStyle* featured it in one of the magazine's first issues. At $15 a bottle—

triple the price of most polish—stores had to ration the stuff. The waiting list was more than a thousand women long.

Vamp became unobtainable, which made it all the more desirable. During that first year, Chanel sold about a million dollars' worth. Not bad for a brand that was only in five hundred stores and a product that was almost always out of stock. Five weeks after Vamp, Revlon launched a lookalike called Vixen. Within months, Chanel spun off a Vamp lipstick, followed by Very Vamp and Metallic Vamp. Dominique found herself doing a color story with a lookalike called Mood Indigo.

For years afterward, women wanted only unusual colors. Young men started wearing strange nail polishes because they thought it made them look like rock stars. Entire businesses were built on the craze for odd, overpriced polish. In 1995, when the Vamp fad was in full swing, Cisco Systems cofounder Sandy Lerner forswore Silicon Valley for the beauty biz. Launching a company called Urban Decay, she went Goth one better with shades like Roach, Smog, and Mildew. The company (slogan: "Does pink make you puke?") sold $6 to $9 million its first year.

That same year, U.S.C. student Dineh Mohajer dumped food coloring in white nail polish to turn it baby blue. Everybody raved. So Dineh borrowed $50,000 from mom and dad and started a business called Hard Candy. Pricing bottles at an exorbitant $18, she offered shades called Hick and Trailer Trash. Within a year, she sold $10 million.

The next year, Revlon jumped in with both feet, launching an entire line of eccentric shades called Street Wear. Urban Decay's founder was incensed, claiming that Revlon copied her idea. Nobody made much mention of Chanel; its backstage improvisation was already ancient history.

Meanwhile, Chanel's makeup artists had moved on. Manicures could not have been more traditional. At one show, nails were painted bright colors that Mademoiselle's own clients might have worn. At the next, nails were pale. They were anything but Vamp. Everybody was catching on to the rich-girl Goth thing. And if the whole world already wants your product, there's no point in putting it on the runway.

"FABULOUS!" André Leon Talley's voice booms over the roar of the blowdryers. With three video cameras recording each epigrammatic overstatement, *Vogue*'s six-foot-six-inch editor-at-large, here to style the Oscar de la Renta show, oracularly utters fashion pronouncements in the manner made famous by his mentor Diana Vreeland. Over by the clothes racks, Oscar himself holds forth to a cable reporter. And, for reasons best known to themselves, a Japanese video crew that's been here since 9:00 A.M. is still contentedly filming the hair crew sipping coffee.

Except for interviews, nothing much is going on. Hair and makeup haven't started. Nobody's dressed. Cameras outnumber models two to one.

"Flash in your face?" a photographer with a foot-high flash attachment says to Linda Cantello. "Are you all right with that?"

"No, actually. I've just woken up," is her ignored reply. By the time she mutters, "They always get you on the worst mornings," his autodrive is on. The minute Linda turns to her first model, another still photographer and three videocameras materialize. Then, bored of waiting their turn for hair and makeup, a couple of models take out their toy-sized Sonys and start videoing. Linda, who went out and bought a Sony yesterday, also has her own man in the media melee. Now, in the media version of a hall of mirrors, he stands in back of the group, pointing a Handicam at the models videoing the press videoing them.

As the assembled audience whirs and flashes and clicks, Linda clutches a mysterious Japanese product whose only English script identifies it as Rubotan Line Liquid and draws a thick black line underneath the girl's eye. Then she doodles three lashes at the outside edge, an effect that manages to evoke Betty Boop, kewpie dolls, and the 1960s Twiggy—without exactly quoting any of them.

Upside-down eyeliner is a strange choice for a designer whose work is so unironic. But it supplies a sexy subtext to all the pale, pretty suits that will be going down today's runway, and it makes you believe that old Oscar is a pretty hip guy, despite doing clothes that fashion magazines caption as "wearable."

More flashes pop. Two cameramen elbow each other to get better close-ups.

Not a look women will be wearing to the mall.

"Perfect! Perfect!" proclaims André, as he sweeps down the hair and makeup aisle, scattering exclamation points in his wake. "I love the eye! Let them all be that way!"

"Genius!" chimes in the head hair stylist.

From the runway, of course, nobody will see any eyeliner. This is all for the benefit of the cameras. "FABU-LOUS!" booms the big voice as Linda moves on to the next girl.

Fashion shows used to be little dinky things: Stories that only made the women's pages. Shows were in showrooms, not stadium-sized venues. In Paris, models walked a narrow aisle between socialite clients and middle-aged editors perched on gilt chairs. In New York, they were more likely to walk between buyers and junior editors and the chairs were less likely to be gilt. In Milan, there weren't any shows at all; Italy's industry was small and showed in Florence.

The models working those long-ago shows were no cover girls. During the 1950s, someone like Christian Dior's beloved Victoire could be a runway favorite when she was still too short, too young, and too quirky to land big bucks advertising. Beautiful black women could walk for Oleg Cassini and Pauline Trigère when no one wanted them on magazine pages. Runway makeup was thick, theatrical, and standardized, like greasepaint worn by a chorus or corps de ballet. Backstage, models had better be prepared to execute their own maquillage. Because makeup artists were few and far between.

Runway didn't pay much either. *Cabine* girls, or house models, were mostly retained on modest monthly salaries. During press presentations, they might make a dozen or more changes (as opposed to today's two or three) and be compensated with a couple of free outfits and introductions to potential husbands. Well into the 1970s, paychecks for the best girls in the biggest shows were hundreds of dollars, not thousands. Nobody made much fuss about American fashion shows anyway. Paris was prestige. Seventh Avenue was shmattes.

Until a few Americans figured out the publicity potential. "Ralph Lauren wanted a consistency of image for his brand, so he wanted Clotilde [the model in his advertising] in his show," explains Katie Ford, of Ford Models. "Suddenly, designers wanted their print models walking their runways." Famous faces brought more attention to the shows, the shows brought more attention to the models, and the whole thing snowballed.

Supermodels came next. Gianni Versace wanted *Vogue* cover girls on his runway and was willing to pay phenomenal sums to get them. Runway paychecks went from three to four to five figures, as designers outbid each other to book the assorted anointed. Claudia Schiffer may have klumpfed down the catwalk like a Clydesdale, but no one cared. Having her in a show was worth millions in publicity.

The minute big money was involved, designers stopped trusting makeup to models. They hired specialists, the same way that they hired D.J.s to mix soundtracks and stylists to play up any literary or historical allusions. Venues were a lot larger, but nobody much cared if makeup read to the back row. Anybody important sat up front. Runway makeup was now created, not for a few socialites in a showroom, but for the media millions represented by bleachers full of photographers with telephoto lenses.

Beauty was soon getting as much attention as fashion. Unlike the clothes, makeup rarely got a bad review. Women found far-out makeup more *amusant* than far-out fashion. It didn't require much self-deprivation or credit-card commitment. It could be washed off at night.

Bigger shows were better for everybody. Models might not have enjoyed cameras and mikes thrust in their faces during morning makeup calls, but they were plenty happy with bigger fees and extra editorial exposure. Television producers loved being able to just turn on a camera and get famous faces for free. Photographers didn't object to guaranteed good money for following young, professionally photogenic women around. And beauty editors far preferred buying runway photos to doing hellishly time-consuming and expensive shoots.

All those runway beauty pictures weren't doing the designers any harm either. They were great spillover publicity for the lines of jeans and shoes and underwear that make the real money. Decades late, it had dawned on designers (and their backers) that the more exciting the runway shows could be made to seem, the more potentially profitable the products linked to them.

And there's easy money to be made. Especially in beauty. Perfume has been subsidizing fashion since the days of Poiret. Other licenses may be lucrative, but they can't match the prestige or profit margins of beauty products. Mademoiselle Chanel may have spent many a night in the atelier ripping and redoing toiles, but Chanel No. 5 made her more money than anything else she ever did. Makeup doesn't do badly either: Walk into a specialty store and watch the traffic at Chanel, Dior, or Yves St. Laurent counters.

Let Carolina Hererra charge a fortune for her outfits. Let Oscar show his stuff on size-two teenyboppers. Any woman can have what she wants from the runways. All she has to do is visit the beauty department.

While they wait for everybody else to show up, the brunette bums a cigarette and tells the makeup crew about the show she just finished. Three of them listen raptly as she regales them with her descriptions of what went down the runway.

Ravaged silver paint covered half of each model's face. "No eyes," she says, with the excitement of a little girl repeating a Stephen King story at a slumber party. "No lips. No cheeks." Features disguised by unsaleable swathes of uncommercial metallic. She makes the show sound like fifteen minutes of a fevered, futuristic trance.

Nothing the magazines will be recommending to their readers. Nothing a woman could ever wear to a party or buy at a mall.

After pumping the model for particulars, the makeup artists are absolutely agog with admiration. "How *fab-u-lous*," one groans in frustration. "Now that's *real* makeup."

Art versus commerce. Purism versus pandering. Makeup *artiste* versus makeup artist.

"Foundation?" shrieks a member of one of the more fashionable makeup crews. "Bobbi Brown uses foundation because she's *selling* foundation." He makes the mandatory shudder of distaste. Foundation is the kind of makeup women wear on the street.

Outside Bryant Park, that's not such a bad thing. Inside, it keeps Bobbi out of the clique lapping up the crème de la crème. As other makeup artists around here will gleefully remind you, she doesn't do Donna or Calvin or Ralph.

But if that bothers Bobbi, she's crying all the way to

the bank. Long ago, she learned there was money to be made for anyone willing to venture outside the realm of runways and supermodels and explain their ways to common folk. In 1991, she and her partner, a public relations executive, put up $10,000 apiece and launched their company at Bergdorf's with ten lipstick shades. Their timing was perfect. Bobbi was not the runway world's most hotshot makeup artist. But no one outside the runway world cared.

Beauty editors adored Bobbi, and covered her lipsticks out of all proportion to the line's size or availability. She started making foundations because women wanted to buy foundations. Soon she was rolling out eye shadows, mascaras, blushes, and brushes and selling them at specialty stores and the Frédéric Fekkai salon (until Frédéric started his own line). Four years later, Lauder acquired the company and the soccer mom became a zillionairess fronting an international brand.

Bobbi, like most makeup artists, almost never wears the stuff herself unless it's for a public appearance, although she never seems to get tired of putting it on other people. She still does a full schedule of shows every season and, if the designers are not all marquee names, well so much the better, since then the publicity stays focused on her. Ever the trouper, she got up at 5:45 this morning to drive in from Jersey for a 7:00 A.M. call. Now, at noon, she's back in the same small tent getting ready to do Steven DiGeronimo, her second of three shows today, and trying to finish her Diet Sprite while a member of her public relations team rigs her with a body mike. She calls home to check on the baby for the umpteenth time, chucks her cell phone into an Hermès bag that cost as much as most moms' cars, then does a touch-up of her lip gloss before the cameras come.

While she waits around, Bobbi plays with pans of eye shadow from Diego Dalla Palma and Lancôme. Both colors, a wine and a dark charcoal, are similar to shades already in her line, except that these have some sparkle. Apparently, though, neither is exactly what she wants. Nevertheless, as she blends and layers and dabs and smudges them across the back of her hand, she blithely announces to a member of her entourage that "These are giving me ideas for fall." Doubtless some fussbudget somewhere will protest that production and distribution time lines make such a late shade launch impossible, but Bobbi doesn't look too bothered by that. "They'll have to get it out," she says, matter-of-fact as a suburbanite telling contractors to finish the kitchen remodeling on time. Then she blends the shadows on the back of her hand and contentedly considers the result.

As the countdown to showtime commences, a public relations minion whisks away the alien powders, then gives them back to Bobbi stripped of incriminating logos and packaging. With cameras ready to roll, it's now Bobbi Brown products as far as the eye can see. Bobbi Brown foundations in bottles and sticks and jars. Bobbi Brown lip liners. Bobbi Brown eye shadows. Bobbi Brown everything else.

Bobbi starts the first model, dabbing foundation on a teenager whose skin doesn't seem to need it. Boxed in by media, Bobbi works away, unfazed by the videocam six inches from her face, the camera a foot behind her head, the guy shooting over her shoulder, or her own videographer and still photographer dancing in the background.

"Talk about fall," barks a middle-aged woman wielding a reporter's notebook.

"Very natural. There are lots of plums and sheers," says Bobbi, always good for the sound bite.

The reporter, beside herself to be interrogating such a celebrity, presses on with the fact-finding mission. "Do you have any help or advice to give women?"

Without a second's hesitation, Bobbi answers: "The first thing is choosing a great foundation."

"Customers come in with runway pictures and say 'What about this look?'" says Debbi Hartley, explaining why she's made the trip to New York this week.

Debbi susses out beauty trends for Nordstrom, where her title is national education director for cosmetics. Like it or not, that means looking at lots of runway makeup. "Runway gets a lot of press," she says, and that has its own momentum: Published pictures influence what women buy, so the magazines publish more of them, so they gain more influence. "Runway" is a magic word for selling makeup.

This week, Debbi will troop around to about a dozen shows. She can't actually see the models' makeup too well from the audience, so her presence is partly pro forma. After the shows are over, she'll buy backstage beauty shots from a forecasting company, go on the Internet to check out the European runways, and cross-examine makeup artists.

As of today, it's too soon to say what the big stories will be—although she already has a few ideas. For example, she likes the "bronzy look" Linda Cantello did at one of the shows. That's the kind of look that can be sold to almost anyone. She's also noticed smoky eyes and berry lips. "Liner is back," she says. "Liner for the eyes. Liner for lips too—because it's hard to do that deep berry mouth without a line to contain it."

Nobody at the shows has been using lip liner. But so what? Women want the runway story. Debbi wants to give it to them.

Like most migratory herds, fashion people sense climate changes long before they occur. Weeks ago, everyone already knew how fabulous Gisele was going to be. In the same way, everyone knows that Tommy will have the most fabulous show. Everyone just knows.

Tonight, Tommy Hilfiger is showing his women's and men's collections in the Roseland Ballroom, the funky dance landmark that rents out as a rock 'n' roll venue. Instead of a taped soundtrack, he's booked the band—

everybody already knows this too—that is next month's cover of *Rolling Stone*. The show isn't scheduled until seven. But by 4:00 P.M. call time, backstage is easily the most fabulous place on the planet. In that casual, off-hand way that somehow makes it even more fabulous.

The fixed point in this turning world, the bartender, stands at the famous Rose Bar pouring an endless supply of Moët & Chandon into an endless supply of plastic champagne coupes while hair and makeup set up around him. Tommy, the man himself, is here getting a quick haircut before the cameras arrive—the Connecticut boy looking, with his baby face framed by the red barber's bib, like he took the wrong turn out of a Norman Rockwell illustration.

The *Vogue* girls are all coming. Alek and Maggie and Trish and Erin and Carmen. And Gisele. (You can't have an event like this without Gisele.) All the music girls are walking for Tommy too. Kidada, the daughter of Quincy Jones. Kimora Lee, the model who married hip-hop zillionaire Russell Simmons. Fifteen utterly fabulous girls.

The utterly fabulous boys walking for Tommy aren't as well known, but a couple of them have arrived early enough to grab a beer and pick up the macho rock 'n' roll vibe. "Yeah, man. I got two skinned-up knees," brags one tough guy in dirty jeans, a torn T-shirt, and an $8,500 Rolex. He and his friend swig Heinekens and snarl, "Let's go smoke cigs before hair and makeup."

Linda Cantello is here early, trying to get the show's

story straight before the cameras descend. She lines a model's eyes Cleopatra-style. Then she stares for a minute. Then she shakes her head.

She tries blending. Pretty soon, all the lines are blended away.

Stymied, she stares at the model for another minute.

Linda roots through a bag and pulls out a little jar of sparkling, sooty powder bearing a mysteriously numbered M·A·C label. Charily, she blackens the lids.

Now the girl looks like Nosferatu.

"Gorgeous!" murmur the makeup crew who's been watching her work.

Tonight, Tommy's story is all about rock 'n' roll. Everyone will be made suitably dark-eyed and decadent—in a Hilfiger-wholesome sort of way. Linda contemplates the model, then brushes some blush on her cheeks to ward off vampire allusions or accusations of heroin chic.

One by one, the makeup artists come by to borrow the magic dust, which Linda dribbles out as carefully as cocaine: Custom-made by M·A·C's professional division, Linda's powder can't be bought for love or money. Tommy's own makeup line is nowhere in sight.

Tonight, the guys get eye goo too. The old rock 'n' roll symbol of rebellion supplying bad-boy spin to Tommy's turtlenecks, topcoats, and suits. One guy, eager to demonstrate that he is not just another mindless male model, tells the makeup artist, "I've read that ants have lifespans of up to sixteen years." She nods and acts very impressed.

Champagne flows faster and faster. Everybody feels more and more fabulous. A very happy Maggie Rizer plops into Linda's makeup chair, and hunts for someplace to park her Moët. "I've had two already!" she announces with a big smile.

"Did you see the front page of the paper today?" one makeup artist asks another, gesturing to the *Daily News*, which has bannered, "My Life in Hell: Supermodel Kate Moss tells of drugs and booze." Inside, the paper carries Kate's first interview since rehab, with the quote "You always have champagne before shows." Kate, last seen strolling Versace's runway with her hair dyed shocking pink, isn't doing New York this season. "Poor thing. She's not in any shows," the second makeup artist replies with a sympathetic shake of the head. Then both of them put down the champagne coupes and get back to work.

With hair and makeup well underway, a few photogenic celebrities are ushered backstage. Then, with all players in position, the doors open so the press can get its candid, unrehearsed stories on the backstage action.

Looking a little lost, Thomas Gibson, the star of TV's *Dharma & Greg*, stands near the buffet with his pretty wife. Out of nowhere, a Tommy Hilfiger executive appears and bellows out: "We've created a whole new language for menswear!"

"Well, thank you for inviting me," the actor replies politely.

"I was like 'GET THEM HERE!'" the man brays before disappearing back into the backstage swirl.

Trailed by a video crew, Tommy Hilfiger does the usual designer procession through hair and makeup. A bodyguard, not much taller than Tommy but as wide and impassible as a wall, hovers just out of camera range. As the video crew documents his creative input, Tommy gestures toward a model's hair and declares, "I just need something more here." Picking up her cue, a makeup artist pretends to fuss with the hair until the camera moves safely past.

As 7:00 P.M. gets closer and closer—and then passes—techies yell their countdown to showtime. "Hair and makeup, we have twenty minutes to first look!"

"In five minutes all camera crews have to leave."

"Male models! First outfits!"

"Clear it out! Everyone out please! NOW!"

With cameras and reporters evicted, the girls strip down to thongs and hurry into their first looks. Linda, champagne coupe in one hand and powder puff in the other, sallies forth to the staging area. Dozens of the makeup artists, hair stylists, and production people, who always pack up and head home at this point, sprint up to Roseland's balcony to catch the action.

At 7:29—only half an hour late—the models are miraculously lined up and ready to go. While Tommy beams beatifically at everyone, a man standing next to him does his best to whip everyone into the requisite frenzy. "BOYS, OWN THE WORLD! GIRLS, WORK YOUR PUSSY!" The boys, juiced on beer and buckets of champagne, whoop back at him.

Out front, it's complete chaos. Three cameramen, who look like they could plunge to their deaths at any second, hang in the air above a huge TOMMY HILFIGER sign. The music is deafening. Photographers' flashes explode like out-of-sync percussion for the band. There's no runway. Models walk right through the audience—a choice that makes the assembled arbiters of chic look pathetically frumpy in comparison to the beered-up boys strutting through their midst in mascara and kilts.

Snuffling, congested Gisele, who's been miserably panting through her mouth up until now, clamps her lips shut in a sultry pout. Snorting through seductively flared nostrils, she strides down the first aisle then hesitates a half second to lower her chin and fire her bombshell pose at the wall of cameras. The photographers go berserk.

Upstairs in the balcony, the normally blasé backstage crews hang over the railings and shove to get a good view. Everybody's hyped about this one. The after-show party is at Brown's. Everybody's going. It's going to be great—everybody already knows.

Down on the floor of Roseland, the band belts out its big hit while Gisele and the other girls glower at the cameras from their black-rimmed rock 'n' roll eyes. Months from now, when all those pictures are published, millions of women will fall in love with this look. Thousands of them will try to re-create it without Linda's little jar of M·A·C powder, then wonder why they just can't get it right.

． ． ．

"Models' breath smells like a camel's ass," moans a makeup artist as he unpacks his breath mints and brushes. "It's the coffee and cigarettes," says another burnt-out case, wrinkling his nose.

Donna Karan's show falls on the Friday of a long week. An 11:30 call comes and goes with no models. No Linda Cantello either. Her crew passes the time gossiping about last night's Tommy Hilfiger after-party, where a married makeup artist made off with one of the male models. "Both," says a leering member of today's crew, "bombed out of their minds."

At 12:15, Stella Tennant, this month's *Vogue* cover girl, arrives, trailed by baby and nanny. Far too fabulous to fuss with her own clothes, Stella, who is rumored to be getting $35,000 per show in Milan this season, wears dirty sneakers, beat-up cargo pants, and two washed-out T-shirts. Plunking herself at a makeup station with aristocratic aplomb, the unmarried granddaughter of the Duke and Duchess of Devonshire hoists both T-shirts and lets the baby have a suck while she rolls herself a ciggie and catches up with the makeup crew.

Linda turns up a few minutes later and settles in for a good gossip with her good friend Stella, although people keep interrupting with annoying questions about the show's makeup. Today's story seems to be that the Donna Karan customer can be simultaneously spiritual and sensual. "Clean matte skin. A little blush. Lipstick,"

Linda shouts out, before turning back to Stella and stage-whispering, "Have you noticed that I make it up as I go along?"

At 1:15, Gisele belts into the room straight from somebody else's show. She wails that the minute this is over, she has to fly to St. Bart's for a shoot. The saga of her cold continues. "Who has tissue? Check this out!" she announces to all, before honking like a giant swan. "My nose is full of stuff!"

No one's makeup is done. A few girls have their hair finished: scraped off their faces into chignons, then skewered by glass rods that look like swizzle sticks. Surveying the scene, the show's producer looks ready to burst into tears. "The show's at four o'clock," Linda says to him in her most soothing, maternal voice.

"No, the show's at three," he says.

Linda mimes an *oops!* without managing to seem very guilty, and turns back to Stella. She takes a mystery lipstick—nobody remembers what it was originally—from one of her homemade palettes. Then she fishes out a lab sample, #434, left over from a consultation she did for Kanebo, a Japanese brand. Tapping a little of each on Stella, she orders "Smack!"

Stella rolls her lips back and forth. The resulting red mouth—a mix of two lipsticks that are not for sale and probably never will be—looks ripe and sexy and all the other things that today's dresses and hairdos definitely do not. Satisfied, Linda shrugs and breaks to phone her husband and kids. Makeup done and baby back with his nanny, Stella rolls herself another cigarette from her pouch of Drum tobacco and smokes it without smudging her lips.

Moët makes the rounds, fueling a furious round of lip-smacking and chignon-skewering. Soon enough, everyone is in the first look: weirdly medieval dresses in rough-weave, religious-habit cloth, with flaps sticking from the skirts like flying buttresses. "How could you walk in this?" wonders one girl, whacking the flap that waggles in front of her. Clustered backstage, they look like a chic pack of penitent nuns.

Once the show starts, the strangeness of the clothes will yield, as it always does, to the glamour of the models, the makeup, and the media frenzy. Gliding past the cameras in their ludicrous dresses and luscious crimson lips, the girls will become, as they always do, gorgeous absurdities. And their makeup will be, as it always is, the most quoted story of the show.

March

ADVERTISING: EVERY PICTURE
TELLS A STORY

THE WOMAN SITTING at the head of the conference table holds up a piece of cardboard that looks like a Rorschach test. Or one of those optical illusions that gives you a headache from trying to take in two things at once.

On the cardboard, two profiles stare confrontationally. The one on the left wears gray makeup, including a gray lipstick that makes her look half-dead. The one on the right wears pink makeup, including pink eye shadow that makes her look as though she's been crying.

The eight people sitting around the table are silent. A couple of brows furrow. They know that this is Revlon's new color story, because that's why they're here this morning. Without captions, though, it's hard to tell what the story is supposed to be. This could be one of those New Age themes. Could be religious (angel of darkness confronts angel of light). Could be science fiction (zombie versus android). Could be almost anything.

"This is 'Thunder and Light,'" the woman running the meeting informs them. The cardboard is a mock-up of the advertising. The space in the center, shaped like the Holy Grail, is where the copy will go.

The little group nods and looks thoughtful.

As this preproduction meeting gets under way, the rest of the fashion and beauty world remains riveted to the Bryant Park shows, which wind up tonight. Less than a mile across town, photographers swarm around makeup artists and models, documenting crimson lips, rock star renderings, smudgy bronzes, and the other stories that will be blazoned all over magazines in a couple of months. This season, as it so often is, runway makeup has been consistently inconsistent. The only story no one seems to be doing is pink and gray.

Revlon will plow on regardless. As will Maybelline and L'Oréal and everyone else stuck with pink and gray stories. Eighteen-month production time lines do not allow for the vagaries of fashion.

For purposes of the "Thunder and Light" campaign, everyone here will proceed as if Revlon is the "fashion authority" touted by its public relations department and gray will be on the lips of the hip this fall. As if Revlon stock, rock bottom right now, is simply undervalued and ready for a turnaround. As if Revlon dominance of the mass market remains unthreatened.

That's the story—and they're sticking to it.

"It's contradictions," declares the woman sitting at the head of the conference table.

She takes out a piece of paper with pink and gray smudges and pushes it to the center of the table so everyone can see the shades. Most of this is for the benefit of Wayne Lucas, the freelance stylist in charge of clothes, jewelry, and anything else needed to get the story across. But it doesn't hurt for everyone else to hear it again.

"We want to push, to make it edgier," the executive explains to the still-silent Wayne.

Last year, when the beauty industry was struggling with the gloomy gray forecast, Revlon, like everyone else, decided to put pink in its lineup. Hence the current color story. The product development people feel it necessary to cite titanium architecture and celebrities in pink clothes as seminal influences. Their concept boards show stormy skies next to shiny Prada suits.

"Originally, we were going to call them 'Thunder and Lightning'—" the executive starts to explain.

"But we brought in 'Light,'" pipes up another employee, "because it's more optimistic."

Nobody adds anything to that one. The executive pulls

out comps that show Cindy Crawford, Revlon's favorite face for the last decade, sashaying toward the camera. On the walls around the room, Cindy's face beams down from framed ads, like the patron saint of lipstick sales. Right now, Cindy's "Q Score," media measure of popularity and instant recognition, is one of the world's highest. Outside this room, everyone whispers that Revlon won't be renewing her contract.

The exec recapitulates: "We'll be covering her close and frontal in two applications." Four photos.

Maybe shooting this on Cindy can help. Of late, the once-mighty Revlon has been an easy mark for the business press. Its stock, once so well valued that crafty old Madame Rubinstein bought it as a joke and kept it as an investment, trades at a fraction of the prices of Avon or Estée Lauder. True, the company still leads the mass market in lipstick sales, although it hasn't advertised Super Lustrous lipstick, its bestselling brand, in years (and won't this year either). According to its public relations department, Revlon is now more interested in positioning itself as a fashion authority.

"The looks coexist. It's not day. It's not evening," someone says. Wayne continues to incline his head and look thoughtful.

The shoot is scheduled eleven days from now. Everything is ready. Makeup. Model. Pose. All that's left is finding the fashion and exposing the film.

Just to make sure Wayne gets the point, another exec repeats: "It's all about contradictions."

. . .

Back in 1952, Revlon's in-house advertising people were stuck with another fall story that was supposed to play on contradictions: "Fire and Ice." The trouble that year was that there weren't any contradictions; there weren't even two colors. The story was plain red lipstick and plain red nail polish. And, even in 1952, those had already been around for a long, long time.

In those days, lead time was ten months instead of eighteen. Not much else was different: Advertising preproduction came in February and the ad was shot in March, same as today. In February, the company had to pick a model without any clue of what clothes she would wear. So they fell back on Dorian Leigh, a thirty-two-year-old brunette who pioneered the Sexy Cindy–brand of commercial sultriness. Dorian had already racked up quite a record with Revlon, beginning with "Fatal Apple" in 1945. No matter what they came up with, she could probably put it across.

Since the makeup was nothing much, Dorian's outfit would have to tell the story. Revlon's people copied a big, dramatic Balenciaga cape in fiery red (the "Fire"), then copied a Norman Norrell halter dress in sparkling white (the "Ice"). On the day of the shoot in March, the gown still didn't have a finished back and the crew was still furiously applying rhinestones. But, by the time Richard Avedon clicked his shutter, enough rhinestones were stuck to the dress to cover the part that showed in the picture. That was all that counted.

In the final ad, Avedon's sensational picture of sexy Dorian ran alongside a quiz that became one of the all-time classics of copywriting. You were "made for Fire and Ice" if you answered yes to eight out of its fifteen questions. ("If tourist flights were running, would you take a trip to Mars?" "Do you close your eyes when you're kissed?")

The company spent in the high six figures of 1952 dollars to run that quiz in every print medium possible. *Vogue* did a "Fire and Ice" issue in exchange for advertising. Other media proved similarly cooperative. Radio stations were blitzed with Revlon-generated quizzes and press releases and opinion polls. The company claims it also got store owners to kick in nine thousand window displays themed to match the ads.

It worked. "Fire and Ice," a color story that was old news even before it came out, remains the most successful and celebrated beauty advertising of all time. A half century later, the color is still selling. Apropos of Dorian, her dress, and the success of "Fire and Ice," Revlon advertising chief Martin Revson pontificated: "Most women lead lives of dullness, of quiet desperation. Cosmetics are a wonderful escape from it—if you play your cards right."

Like big brother Charles, who had founded the company, Martin Revson never shied away from sounding condescending, particularly if he was talking about women. "You have to sell by touching all the facets of the emotional side of a woman," he told the business press. In the "Fire and Ice" era, clothes were the usual place to start. They still are.

Package design is a picnic compared with this. When a company picks packaging it can hedge its bet by testing on focus groups. Picking clothes is pure crapshoot. Potential customers might not have opinions about the beveled versus straight-edged corners on compacts, but every last one of them has an opinion about clothes. Show one woman a twinset and she calls it classic. Show the same sweaters to her sister and she calls them dowdy.

So Revlon is now doing what all the other beauty companies do. It has hired a high-powered stylist: Wayne. He will be the one who fleshes out the concept on those computer-generated cardboards. Like a writer-for-hire who spins the concept into a screenplay, his job will be getting the story across.

To do that, he begins by wrangling as many designer outfits out of showrooms as possible. Then, to round out the selection, he and his crew comb stores for "directional merchandise," meaning fashion that will still look fashionable six months from now.

Hence this afternoon's meeting. And why the conference room at Tarlow, Revlon's in-house advertising agency, looks like the back room at Loehmann's. On four jammed clothes racks, crudely handmade sweaters hang next to dainty sequin-speckled twinsets, crisp summer cottons next to heavy winter wools, and sporty skirts spout elegant formal trains. The pick also includes a pin-striped suit with steel studs and an evening gown made out of chain mail. To communicate contradictions, this is a good start.

"Wayne always brings a mountain of stuff," says an ad exec as she trips over a shopping bag. While she settles in for what looks to be a long haul, one of Wayne's assistants spreads a clean cloth on the conference table and covers it with necklaces: fake pearls in grays and pinks, rhinestones glistening on a cobweb of wire, a sadistic-looking gorget of torched plastic, a swirl of feathers suspended on fish line and cantilevered like a Calder mobile.

T-shirts and shawls blanket every other surface, some still with price tags from Barneys and Bergdorf's. Rejected garments will be returned. Used or damaged merchandise comes out of the shoot budget.

Commissioned pieces fill the blanks between showrooms and stores: a vest knit out of transparent plastic cord, more jewelry made of plastic. And, should someone have a brilliant idea today, Wayne has crews standing by to execute everything in time for Tuesday's shoot.

Most of this stuff is unusable. Clothes are here to be copied, created, or dyed. Lined if they are too sheer. Lengthened if they are short. Shortened if they are long. Flipped inside out if the right side is too shiny on camera. Sequinned if they are not. Sleeves ripped out. Sleeves sewn on.

Once all the execs find a chair not covered with accessories, a beautiful brunette appears in the doorway wearing a sleeveless gray gown. Booked as a dress-up doll for the next two hours, Pseudo-Cindy comes complete with brown eyes, olive skin, longish hair, and 34B bust. Her job is to stand there and let everyone stare. After she does that for a silent minute or so, a Tarlow exec ventures "Very nice."

Still, it's not *quite* right.

Discussion ensues. A Polaroid is taken. Polaroids, the preferred means of notation in the fashion world, will be this meeting's aide-mémoire. No one here sketches. No one takes notes.

Pseudo-Cindy reappears in a sweet, smocked gown.

Too *Romeo and Juliet*.

White chiffon with rivulets of sequins that look like currents of lightning?

Maybe. It would have to be dyed. (The Polaroid whirs.)

A sheath that looks like it's made of shrink wrap?

Fun, but not right.

Discussion and recapitulation. The agency exec picks up the plastic-cord vest that has fascinated her from the beginning and fingers it thoughtfully. "This could be 'Light,'" she says.

A bolero made of black marabou?

"Too L'Oréal."

This cardigan?

The real Cindy doesn't like cardigans.

Deep sighs all around the table. Can it be a coincidence that Clinique, the bestselling brand in department stores, advertises without showing models or clothes?

A wifebeater tank top worn with a satin skirt?

"Too Marlon in *Streetcar*."

One gown is insufficiently dramatic.

Another is "too disco-y."

After an hour and a half of this, a Revlon exec takes the pile of Polaroids and spreads them out like tarot cards. Diet Cokes pop open. Pepperidge Farm cookies are passed around. Wayne stares long and hard at the mock-ups of the ads and listens to everybody put in her two cents.

"I hear you," he says.

"I'm with you," he says.

"It could be beautiful."

As the dress parade resumes, the team rejects anything "too close to what people would be wearing."

A tweed top with a cowl neck?

No.

A sheath with bra straps showing?

Nope, not right either.

One Revlon exec passes Wayne swipe of some outfits she's especially liked. Nodding as though he's happy for the input, Wayne looks it over patiently and says, "We'd have to have that made."

Trying to get across the mood of the season, he explains: "What they're doing for fall . . . no one is doing pretty anymore."

. . .

Do so many stories about beauty sound the same because they share hidden meanings? Or is it because they
share some common origin? Harriet Hubbard Ayer
could be used to make either point.

Long before Hedy Lamarr or Paulette Goddard
touted Max Factor, even before Alice Roosevelt Long-
worth and Queen Marie of Romania advertised Pond's
or Lillie Langtry pushed Pear's, there was Harriet, acting as her own celebrity spokesmodel. And that was
only one of her distinctions. Harriet was also a pioneer
as tycoon, huckster, copywriter, beauty editor, industry
booster, and cautionary tale.

Born in 1849 into a Chicago family better endowed
socially than emotionally, she took advantage of her
good looks to get married and out of the house at sixteen. After losing a child, a home, and very nearly her
life in the Great Chicago Fire, she headed for Paris to
recover. There, on the Boulevard Malesherbes, she discovered a perfumer, Monsieur Mirault, who regaled her
with stories of the cosmetic his father and grandfather
brewed for Juliette Récamier, the legendary beauty of
the Directoire.

Back in Chicago, Harriet pulled herself together and
became a society hostess, showing off the Worth gowns
she'd picked up in Paris and entertaining Adelina Patti
and Oscar Wilde when they passed through town.

However, as so often seems to happen with women who wind up as beauty tycoons, she was able to make a success of everything except marriage. In 1886, Harriet moved to New York, where she was soon supporting herself and her children by advising the *nouveau riche* on antiques and other niceties.

When a client named Jim Seymour offered to stake her, Harriet took $50,000 seed money (in exchange for stock), bought the Récamier formula, invested in gorgeous glass jars so she could repackage it under her own name, and began to advertise. Harriet wrote ads that were fairy stories for grown-up girls, dropping names of clients like Patti, the opera diva, and the Princess of Wales, discoursing on the legendary looks of Madame Récamier and her influence on French history, telling tales of miraculous makeovers that begot marriage proposals from rich and handsome men. Business took off immediately.

All was going swimmingly until 1889, when Harriet wound up in court. She charged that Seymour, her backer (and now a relative through her daughter's marriage), was trying to drive her insane so he could take over her company. Harriet said Seymour was out for revenge because she had repelled his physical advances. The robber baron may indeed have made advances but her luscious business was the more likely lust object. The trial was the talk of New York. Harriet's notoriety skyrocketed. So did her sales.

She won that battle, but not the war. A few years later,

Seymour did succeed in getting Harriet carted off to the looney bin. As a good-looking woman who ran her own business when she could have easily found a spouse to support her, Harriet's sanity was already suspect. Eventually Harriet escaped incarceration, so her story went, with the aid of a mysterious Freemason to whom she communicated her plight in coded French.

Whether or not that was true, when she emerged fourteen months later, her company had been taken away. Harriet was forty-five, fresh out of the asylum, abandoned by her family, and broke. Undaunted, she fell back on beauty once again. With no writing experience except the stories spun in those long-winded ads, she convinced Joseph Pulitzer to put her on his newspaper. She now became America's first beauty editor.

By the time she died at age fifty-four, Harriet had become a vocal, visible advocate of women's rights. She joined the Rainey Daiseys, a group who wore skirts a shocking four inches off the ground for the sake of safety and sanitation. She favored plain-front corsets over the deforming wasp waist.

Yet Harriet went to her grave convinced that the beauty business was the best thing to ever happen to American women. According to her, beauty products boosted more than mere vanity: An economic upheaval following the Civil War was forcing women out of their homes and into the workplace, where a better appearance translated into increased employability. As she put it, "Not all of them liked it, but they were quick to find out that youth and good looks gave them an advantage over plainer rivals." In Harriet's view, women needed all the help they could get.

By the time Charles Revson got into the act in 1932, men had long since taken over mass-market beauty.

Around 1910, when it became obvious that there was serious money to be made, more men started getting into the beauty business. Men couldn't infiltrate the girly, just-between-us atmosphere of the high-end salons, but in the mass market, being male was a big advantage. Distribution channels were an old boy network of pharmacists and mostly male store owners. Men also had an easier time attracting investors. Mass meant volume, making the price of entry prohibitive to female entrepreneurs. The single disadvantage was that a man—with the possible exception of movie artist Max Factor—couldn't muster the innate authority of a woman on the matter of makeup. And Factor, alas, had an Old Country accent so thick it amounted to a speech impediment.

So the men turned to advertising. Companies like Armand, Bourjois, Maybelline, Max Factor, and Primrose House spent millions promoting their products with ads that were usually written by female copywriters hired solely on fashion and beauty suffrage (and who, in turn, often invented "in house" female experts,

the same way they invented Aunt Jemima to sell pan-
cake mix). All this advertising further increased the
cost of doing business, making it harder yet for women
to crack mass.

Revson wouldn't have been able to crack the mass
market either, if he hadn't resorted to a traditional feminine gambit: starting in salons, then segueing to retail.
The son of Russian-Jewish immigrants, he was born in
1906, grew up in a New England factory town, graduated from high school at age sixteen, and immediately lit
out for New York, where he landed a job on Seventh Avenue. Fashion was his higher education; Revson remained a garmento to the end of his days, forever at
odds with the fancy-schmantzy college boys who ended
up working for him.

In 1931, he was doing salon distribution for a New
Jersey company that made opaque nail polish—a novelty
in the days when polish was streaky, translucent, and limited to two or three colors. Revson called the product
"cream enamel," experimented on himself, and ended up
being able to do better nails than any *koorva* manicurist.
When the company turned down his request for national
distribution, he and his older brother Joseph got together $300 and went halfsies on a venture with a nail
chemist named Charles Lachman (represented by the
"L" in the new company's name).

Revson romanced his new product as hard as if he was
still selling dresses, giving the enamels *sheyne* names and
coming out with new shades twice a year. Sudan one

season, Fifth Avenue Red the next. As much as anything ever dreamed up by Harriet or Madame or Miss Arden, Revlon polish was aspirational from the get-go. His first consumer ad, which ran in *The New Yorker* in 1935, said that Revlon was "originated by a New York socialite." By 1939, he offered matching lipsticks (his claim to the invention of the color story). After that, he was unstoppable.

By the mid-1950s, Revson was running the show single-handedly. Lachman had retired to enjoy his money. Brothers Joseph and Martin could no longer stand working with brother Charles. Famous for pronouncements like "I don't meet competition. I crush it!" Revson reveled in his reputation as a rat bastard. Firing account executives was something of a hobby. At one point, he ran through seven ad agencies in less than three years.

But advertise he did. In the 1950s, a woman named Hazel Bishop developed an "indelible" lipstick. (Nothing new even then: "Kiss-proof" lipsticks were around since World War I.) Outraged that a woman was outselling him in the lipstick market, Revson determined to outspend her. Bishop put up a good fight, but she eventually lost the battle—and her company. (The final insult came in the 1990s when Revlon co-opted her slogan, "Stays on you, not on him," to push its ColorStay lipstick.)

Bishop wasn't the only one to lose control. A generation of doughty old divas, like Madame and Miss Arden, died out, as old age and ill health had pushed the others, like Estée and Mary Kay Ash, into retirement. Today, the world's twenty biggest beauty companies are headed by men, with the exception of Avon, which put a woman into the top spot only recently.

Like lots of good stories, the one about the beauty business being run by women isn't entirely wrong. But it's not entirely true either.

.

Revson really invented the modern cosmetics ad. Up until then, beauty advertising had spelled out stories in copious detail—à la Harriet Hubbard Ayer. Revson let the picture tell the story.

That, in turn, led to the first beauty "faces." Without much copy to spell out the differences between companies, the kind of ads that Revson invented relied on models and styling to supply a subtext. The model's face, her hair style, and the length of her skirt told customers as much about the color story as her makeup. Finding a model who could represent the right message wasn't easy, so companies often found themselves reemploying the same girls. Dorian Leigh did "Fatal Apple," "Fire and Ice," "Cherries in the Snow," and a slew of other successful color stories starting in the 1940s. When Dorian moved to Europe in the mid-1950s, her younger sister, Suzy Parker, took over the gig. Suzy starred in so many campaigns that she thought she deserved some sort of contract. Revson didn't. Nor did he particularly enjoy employing Suzy after she'd had the temerity to ask for appropriate compensation.

Finally, in 1973, Revson bowed to the inevitable and put Lauren Hutton under contract as the face of his Ultima II line, thus initiating yet another tradition in beauty advertising. Playing up the contract as the first exclusive in the history of cosmetics, Revson got publicity worth much more than Hutton's salary (a coup not lost on competitors, who started signing their own models to exclusives). After five months of negotiation, Revson agreed to pay Hutton $200,000 a year for two years. Big money in those days, chump change compared to what came after.

In 1977, Margaux Hemingway signed for $1 million to represent Babe fragrance and cosmetics for the next five years. Then Cheryl Tiegs signed a Cover Girl contract that paid $1.5 million over five years. Isabella Rossellini got $2 million from Lancôme. By the time Cindy Crawford signed her first contract with Revlon, her base pay was $4 million for four years.

For models, a cosmetics contract is the ultimate score. A beauty company buys a specified number of her working days—currently, fifteen days a year is standard—with provisos built into the contract in case more days are needed. The usual contract is two years, and gives the client three one-year options to renew.

If a girl wants to change her hair color or her hair length, she can't do it without notifying the client. She has to watch her weight, because if her body changes too drastically, the whole deal may be off. She also has to mind her Ps and Qs because every contract has a morals clause. "Most of these girls understand that once they get a beauty contract—or any contract—they have to be really careful," says one agent.

Besides buying a model's work, the beauty company also buys her inaction. Like the federal government paying a farmer to keep his fields fallow, the beauty company pays for its "face" not to be seen using products from rival companies, or patronizing certain spas, or appearing in print in anything but its products. Ergo, when any fashion magazine does a shoot starring model Carolyn Murphy, the caption next to her photo must read that all her makeup is by Estée Lauder, regardless of whatever mix of makeup was actually used on the set.

Buying faces, like running those big, glossy, luscious-looking ads that don't say much, has been standard practice for decades. Naomi Kates of Next Models, who's been negotiating the beauty contracts at her agency for ten years, says, "Beauty is such a huge business that no one questions the need for paying models anymore."

If a customer comes into the store and likes what she sees on the placard, she's suddenly in the mood to buy. And, as Kates likes to remind her clients during negotiations, "At least 70 percent of people buy their beauty products purely on impulse."

The flip side is that, when the color story is a stinker, the model is usually the one who's blamed.

Cindy's still-considerable public probably loves her as much for the way she acts as the way she looks. At the apogee of supermodel mania, when Naomi Campbell was constantly, cavalierly four or five or six hours late for jobs, and Linda Evangelista managed to alienate everybody by saying, "We don't wake up for less than $10,000 a day," sensible Cindy made a point of showing up on time. Whenever she opened her mouth in public, she pointed out that the stresses of supermodel-dom compared quite favorably with the stresses of her pre-modeling gigs, which included detasseling corn in De Kalb, Illinois, for minimum wage. She even sounded grateful when she said it.

Today, prompt as ever, she arrives on time for her 8:30 A.M. call, barefaced, utterly lovely, and dressed (skirt, sweater, camel coat) as if she's headed to a business meeting.

Everybody air kisses—*smack! smack!*—everybody else like it's old home week. Everyone knows each other here. One Revlon employee yawns. "My God, doesn't it feel like we just did this?"

Once the greetings are over, the rest of the day is hurry up and wait. On most beauty shoots, it takes at least two hours to get the model ready. A photographer is considered fast and lucky if he finishes his first shot before noon.

Today's photographer, Michael Thompson, hasn't arrived yet. But his crew has been here since eight, getting everything ready. The big diffused lights known as "soft boxes" are rigged. The Pentax cameras are loaded and ready to go.

Wayne and his crew started setting up even earlier. In

one corner of the huge, garage-sized studio, they've improvised a complete dressing room with a full-length mirror, two ironing boards, a steamer, and a seamstress installed in front of a full-sized sewing machine. They've hauled in three "coffins," the long black trunks that stylists use to carry clothes and gear, each one open and at the ready, crammed with contingency supplies like "Assorted Nude Pantyhose," "G-strings," and "Assorted Black Bras" (subdivided by cup size).

Wayne is ready for anything. The comps show Cindy from the knees up, so shoes probably won't be needed. But Wayne has seven pairs of Prada and Manolo Blahnik in size 9 1/2. Just in case. And he has more shoes on the way. Since this ad is for eye shadow, there's no chance they'll need sunglasses either. But Wayne has thirty-two pairs ready. Just in case.

Yesterday, at a 9:00 A.M. meeting at Revlon headquarters, Cindy edited the clothes along with Wayne and the head of advertising. So only eighty-five hangers' worth of outfits have made it to the studio this morning. Along with twenty-seven necklaces. The strange vest made out of plastic cord. Three more of those torched gorgets. Thirteen bracelets. And two hair clips.

All for four pictures. Two of them are close-ups that won't show more than an inch of collar. If that.

Over at the makeup table, the makeup artist chats with Cindy while brushing on the Light lipstick. Cindy chats right back without moving her lips.

A few of the female executives carry on fitful conversation. Which always seems to be about beauty products. In short bursts, they compare stores and prices. "No lip liner! Who knew? It changed my life!" one woman declares with great fervor. Then they all go back to waiting.

Demonstrating why she gets over a million a year for this, Cindy emerges wearing the all pink makeup. On her, it actually looks good. Finally, at a few minutes after 11, Cindy is on set wearing the vest knit out of plastic cord. With the help of folding screens, the photographer's assistants have created a nine-by-ten-foot studio within the studio. Almost a dozen people are crowded into it: the photography team on one side, the Revlon people plus their styling crew on the other. A Revlon employee approaches one of the onlookers and, exceedingly diplomatically, requests that she gawk at Cindy a little less blatantly. Especially "any time you're in her direct line of vision." Cindy doesn't like to be stared at.

With each click of the camera shutter, the big lights make their synchronized pop gun noise. *Pop. Pop.* Again and again and again. Cindy sits in the center on an overturned wooden crate as the photographer moves around her, shooting Polaroids to check the lighting, the exposure, the pose, the hair, the makeup.

From that first *pop*, the mood in the studio changes. Things are serious now. The photographer interrupts himself at one point to discuss, in deadly earnest, the two or three hairs in front of Cindy's left ear. A powwow establishes that the hairs are too short to slick back without lots of goop that would show in the picture.

The makeup artist crouches in one corner in a sprinter's starting position, muttering directions to herself and clutching a compact and brush with a bag of makeup by her side—even though the studio's huge makeup table is less than fifteen feet away. Any time the photographer pauses, even for a second, she darts in to comb Cindy's eyelashes or make some other infinitesimal adjustment.

After ten minutes of this, the photographer huddles with Cindy to examine the Polaroids. Wayne calls for a roll of duct tape and duct-tapes the back of the plastic in place. Still not right. So Wayne flattens himself on the floor behind Cindy and holds the collar in place with his fingertips.

By half past 11, the lights have been fine-tuned and Cindy perches on the beat-up wooden crate, resplendent in her plastic cord and duct tape. Wayne's fingers are pressing into the back of her neck, the business end of a lens is only a few inches from her face, blinding lights are flashing in her eyes, and a dozen people are staring at her as though their livelihoods depended on it.

Cindy looks as relaxed as if she's home lolling in a warm bath. *Pop.* She looks straight into the lights. *Pop.* She tilts her head back and lets her lids slide down a little, projecting pure sexual bliss while—*pop*—showing more of the shadow.

Pop. Pop. The photographer shoots so fast that the sound is relentless, a parody of a war movie. *Pop. Pop. Pop.* The lights synchronized to go off with the shutter are so bright that everyone around Cindy squints as they watch.

Pop. Cindy sits perfectly still. *Pop. Pop.* The heroine of this story doesn't even blink.

May

THE MAGAZINES: TRUTH IS
STRANGER THAN FICTION

AS MAY SUNSHINE soaks Manhattan and streets spill over with grinning women in brand-new summer outfits, magazine editors hole up in their offices and brood about fall.

In a block-sized building catty-corner from Grand Central Station, Linda Moran Evans works in a cubbyhole surrounded by pictures of her nine-year-old in his soccer uniform and messy piles of products and press releases. As an editor at *Family Circle*, Linda probably has the biggest readership of anyone covering beauty and, because she has a proportional print run, is usually the first to go to press.

At the moment, though, neither distinction does her

much good. Linda has to start her fall story soon, the one where she tells twenty-two million readers what's coming from the big beauty companies. Trouble is, the big beauty companies haven't told her. Despite finishing "Winter Beach" six months ago, Lauder hasn't shown it to anybody yet. Avon, Lancôme, L'Oréal, and half a dozen others are being just as uncommunicative.

Linda lets out a shallow, not-quite-silent sigh, a sound she seems to make a lot. She's used to this. Companies know the magazine deadlines and, although they spend fortunes pandering to the press and advertising, they never seem able to get their products across town in time. She's learned not to let it stop her.

Last week she went ahead and got her ideas okayed by the editorial powers that be. A couple of days ago she confirmed a photographer. And tomorrow she'll cast four models, book the hair stylist, makeup artist, and studio, then start calling in clothes and props.

Regardless of what colors the companies are secretly cooking up, Linda's got her own story to get across. Every magazine does. Even this far in advance, it's a safe bet that fall makeup will have a sexy slant in *Cosmo*, a celebrity angle in *InStyle*, and a runway tie-in on the pages of *Marie Claire*.

So, come September, no matter what the beauty companies are offering, everything is going to be wearable, beautiful, and easier than ever on the pages of *Family Circle*.

No matter what it takes.

. . .

A storyteller who specializes in a certain genre usually stays within certain parameters. For a huge cosmetics company like Revlon, the plot devices are far-fetched and the stock characters are million-dollar supermodels like Cindy. For a huge service magazine like Linda's, the stories have to stick closer to the norm and so do the women in them.

In terms of today's casting, that means trying to use black and Asian models instead of the same old blondes. Hiring a thirty-five-year-old instead of a teenager. And trying to track down a woman who looks realistically curvy, but can still squeeze into the samples sent by manufacturers.

Casting models only sounds glamorous to people who don't have to do it. In the industry it's considered a special kind of hell: The kind where, like Tantalus, your heart's desire remains so near and yet so far.

Castings everywhere follow the same format: The girl—and a model is always a "girl" even if she's sixty—comes in with her portfolio. Whoever's doing the hiring looks her over and flips through her book. They take her card, a postcard-sized picture printed with stats like bra cup and shoe size. If it's a runway casting, they watch her walk. Otherwise, she's Polaroided and sent on her way. While this goes on, the model listens to herself being discussed like livestock on the auction block, and has about as much control over her immediate fate.

Linda likes girls "to have a little meat on their bones" and avoids any too thin, too fresh, or too young. She won't cast under twenty-five, which means most modeling agencies have nothing for her. She generally ends up using Ford's Classic division, a couple of agencies that book actresses, and one that specializes in over-the-hill superstars who never would have been caught dead doing *Family Circle* in their heyday. Basically, she wants "sexy-wholesome": someone who looks like everybody's prettiest neighbor—only maybe a little prettier. In Manhattan, she might as well be looking for a unicorn.

Because her beauty shots need someone who can smile and keep her eyes open at the same time, Linda also has to ask, "Can you smile?" and do a surreptitious check of the teeth. She also sneaks a look at the hands to see if she's got a nail-biter who will need a manicurist. Even then she's not home free. Everybody in the business has tales of tattoos, shaved eyebrows, and other misguided modifications that models have been inspired to make in their appearance. The time the clothes didn't fit because the girl got a boob job in between trying them on and arriving at the shoot. The brunette who showed up blond. The haircut that turned Rapunzel into Prince Charming.

Once, when casting for a makeover story, Linda got a man dressed as a woman. She didn't use him.

Sitting behind a Formica table around the corner from her office cubbyhole, Linda has girded herself for today's ordeal in a no-nonsense pantsuit—adding her own spin, as *Family Circle* might say, with a Bakelite doggie pin, a headband, and a natural redhead's full complement of freckles. After ten years at this job, forty-three-year-old Linda still frets about the magazine's forty-five-year-old working mom reader as if she's a real person instead of a statistical composite. Letting out that little sigh again, she asks for the first girl to be sent in.

"I'm forty-six," blurts the model, who could pass for a girl of forty. Flustered, she babbles about her bookings while Linda listens, flips pages, murmurs, "very nice," and hands back the book.

The next one comes from Ford Classic. Linda likes her. But she's blinking in the Polaroid. They take another. The model blinks again. Linda gives up, says, "Great!" and lets her go.

Teenagers turn up, their books full of edgy shots taken in Europe. Some girls are the right age but the wrong look. One blonde won't do because she's already in too many of the magazine's ads. Another blonde won't work because they used her in the same story last year. So far the agencies haven't sent any blacks or Asians, but they have enough blue-eyed blondes to repopulate a Reich.

Some girls forget their cards. Some don't have cards. Some carry cards to promote husbands or children who model too.

Throughout, Linda remains ridiculously polite, as if she could singlehandedly compensate for all rejection endured by all models everywhere. She never comes right out and asks how old the model is. Instead it's "What age category do you work in?" She finds some excuse to say "very nice" during each and every encounter, even if she hates the portfolio. The models smile back and look happy.

Linda waits until a smiling model is safely on the elevator before she stops sounding like Pollyanna. "Too mean" is the verdict about one girl who carries a portfolio full of scowls intended to project sexy intensity. "Too strong," is the verdict about a Miss Bushy Brows who mistakenly thinks her look is fetchingly farouche. Another girl is stunning in person but "looks like her own evil twin" in pictures.

"I'm old and I'm new," announces a girl who took a fifteen-year break "to do a couple of television commercials."

"When the light is right," one thirty-something volunteers, "I can look really, really young. A teenager."

Another old favorite "has put on some weight since we last saw her." At *Family Circle*, this is high praise. Alas, she's been in the magazine too much lately.

Linda nods, turns pages, takes cards, says "very nice" again and again and again.

"My name is Inka. Inka Dinka Do!" the next blonde sings out. "That's what they used to call me."

"That's nice," says Linda, who is looking a little woozy by now.

Inka is led off to be Polaroided. Linda flips through

the book, murmurs, "very nice," hands it back, and says, "thank you"—the model's cue to exit.

Inka waves bye-bye. "Inka Dinka Do!" she chirps one last time.

"Oh my," Linda says, "I think I need some coffee."

A company has its story. A magazine has its story. When the two differ too much, genteel war ensues. A battle for supremacy waged with goody bags, spa stays, and ad contracts.

With practiced public relations that must make entertainment, politics, fashion, organized crime and other image-conscious industries weep with envy, beauty companies subject the ladies of their press to a round of lunches and launches so relentless that the editors barely have time to think. Almost every day, the beauty editor has a working lunch with a PR rep who picks up the check at the Four Seasons or Michael's or 44 or whatever the favored meeting place of the moment might be. At the conclusion of these tête-à-têtes, the hostess invariably hands over a goody bag: a small shopping bag stuffed with products and promotional items. The poor beauty editor is also subjected to endless product presentations, à la Neutrogena's January shindig. (Goody bags a given.) New day spas and salons. (Goody bags or gift certificates.) Store openings. (Goody bags, gift certificates, or "permanent discounts.")

Naturally, not every editor gets the same treatment: There's a rigid hierarchy, and Linda's at the bottom of it. "It's because we don't have a woman on our cover," Linda explains.

"Prestige" is a roundabout reference to every company's favorite editorial credit: The one on the table of contents page that's slugged "cover look" and is followed by a list of products. In the world of beauty PR, *Vogue* is the big score, followed by a short list that includes *W*, *Harper's Bazaar*, *Elle*, and, in an occasional sop to populism, *Glamour* and *InStyle*. Linda may have more readers than *Vogue*, *W*, *Harper's Bazaar*, and *Elle* combined, but she's in the same situation as the blockbuster author who watches literary glory go to obscure poets. Circulation isn't everything. Cover credits are.

For the beauty editor with a cover credit at her disposal, torrents of goody bags inundate the office each day. When any company does a new color story, she gets a sample (which doesn't always arrive in time for her deadline, but that's another story). Often as not, the sample comes squired by a witty gift so she'll feel more obligated to mention it. For example, when Maybelline does a color story using fruity names, a crate of out-of-season fruit and a Braun juicer arrive along with its lipsticks.

Whatever the beauty editor doesn't want (usually the lipsticks) goes into the locked-door stash of leftovers known as the beauty closet. Around the office, much clout derives from her status as keeper of the closet, and dispensation of products is one of the major perks of her job. (Every magazine has a fashion closet too. Unfortunately, designers like their fur coats and cashmere sweaters returned after the photo shoots.)

Then there are the mandatory junkets. Yet another trip to the Golden Door or Canyon Ranch or Green Valley. Individual trips, like the company that flies her to the South Pacific because they're launching Polynesian-themed products. Group jaunts, like the stay in Monaco to celebrate the launch of a perfume. The days in London to inspect Unilever headquarters. Or Paris to inspect L'Oréal laboratories, where she is handed a fistful of francs and parked in a $1,200-a-night room at the Hotel Bristol "to make a nice change from the Ritz." Then back to Paris—is there no respite?—to inspect Guerlain, where LVMH chairman Bernard Arnault fetes his latest fragrance in a national museum amidst Renoirs and Cézannes and Monets. Since the cosmetic company picks up her tab, a beauty editor flies business class when she doesn't fly first. Accommodations are gratis. As are meals. And never forget the goody bag.

Editorial mentions of any size earn the editor, at the very least, a bouquet from the grateful manufacturer. What else it's worth is calibrated according to both the magazine's prestige and the manufacturer's. The mesdames of *Vogue* and *Elle* rate the best loot. However, if the mention was accorded to a major advertiser—someone like Estée Lauder, L'Oréal, or Chanel—a simple thank-you is thought to suffice, since the company already "supports" the magazine through its advertising contract and, in effect, contributes to the editor's salary.

According to the same etiquette, a nonadvertiser is expected to cough up. Appropriate appreciations being a pricey addition to an editor's orchid collection, or a $1,000 gift certificate to Saks Fifth Avenue (dispatched directly to an editor's home in the interest of discretion). Very, very good mentions—the kind that put a business on the map—have meant as much as a Cartier watch or a pair of Angela Pintaldi emerald earrings.

Perks also pour in predictably at year's end. In a seasonal ritual of shrewd public relations, any company with any hope of ever being favorably mentioned in a magazine sends proof of its affections during Christmas, a season that starts with Thanksgiving and ends with Epiphany. An editor-in-chief gets good stuff too; but, for sheer volume, beauty loot beats all. The beauty department fills with robin's egg blue boxes from Tiffany's, orchid plants, bottles of champagne, and cashmere mufflers.

Public relations firms pushing clients without big ad budgets give the best presents. They have to. One company keeps the editorial mentions coming by giving away Prada goodies at Christmas time, always a sure bet with the beauty crowd. Any editor who misses mentions is off the Prada list. A cooperative editor is worth, at the very least, a Prada tote.

Advertisers buy coverage cheaper. Again, competition for ad contracts is enough to keep them in editorial good graces. For form's sake, they send bouquets, scarves, fruit baskets, bottles of wine, or—considered the ultimate in cheesiness—a bottle of their own perfume. However, as with so many things, it was even better in the old days. Up until a decade or two ago, when a fall-off in fashion advertising gave greater prominence to beauty, fur coats, television sets, and ten-speed bicycles still figured prominently on Christmas loot lists. Helena Rubinstein would load herself down with her least-favorite jewelry before being interviewed, so she could take off a bauble and present it to the beauty editor as a spontaneous gesture of affection.

No one questions whether courting the editors is worth the trouble. Of course it is. Magazine mentions put companies like M·A·C and Bobbi Brown on the map. A few years later, they did the same for a slew of newer companies like Hard Candy and Stila.

Even a throwaway mention can push a product right off the shelves. Let *Glamour* feature a gadget called the Topsy Tail, and its inventor gets $100,000 worth of orders in three weeks. Let Sharon Stone tell *InStyle* she favors a certain Chanel concealer, and it sells out nationwide. Beauty history abounds with similar examples.

"The Investigators go behind the scenes to uncover some less-than-model behavior," teases the television announcer, conjuring lurid visions of models and misdeeds. Tonight a top-rated New York news show promises to divulge, "Why you can't duplicate the look you see in magazines."

Toward the end of the newscast, a "former beauty editor" (meaning someone off the Christmas loot list and therefore with nothing to lose) appears silhouetted in the manner of a Mafia informant. She reveals that most magazines give editorial credits where they're not due. Advertisers have preference. Cover credits have nothing to do with the makeup used on the shoot and everything to do with how much money the beauty company spends advertising in the magazine. To get the other side of the story, the reporter interviews Bobbi Brown, who sanguinely says: "That's the nature of the business" and doesn't bother to contradict her.

Computer retouching comes under scrutiny next. As an instance of retouching gone haywire, the report shows a picture of a swimsuited Cindy Crawford in which the divine Cindy's belly button has been computer-eliminated. The report concludes by wondering "why the Federal Trade Commission hasn't investigated."

Next morning, the earnest exposé is already forgotten. No consumer group pickets beauty counters. No company modifies its ads. No magazine changes its cover credits. Business doesn't slow by so much as a single lipstick.

Apparently the revelation that beauty pictures are fantasies and beauty stories are fiction shocks no one. The exposé might as well have been about Santa Claus.

. . .

June *Vogue* hits the stands, with one of those fairy-tale portraits of Nicole Kidman on the cover. Gowned in silk and decked in diamonds, the actress swans through a period setting in a pose straight out of John Singer Sargent.

On the all-important cover credit, her alabaster skin and ruby lips are credited to Clarins. Ten pages later, a full-page Nordstrom ad illustrates every last one of the products purportedly used on the cover—along with convenient ways to order them.

Nordstrom clinched the advertising tie-in before anyone knew who was going to be on the cover, and it's delighted. Lots of women are gonna love this one. "So many customers want the colors on a cover," the store buyer points out, "and a change of lipstick is an inexpensive way of updating your look." Whereas most customers attempting Nicole's storybook aura might find the price of her designer gown and diamond choker a bit beyond their budgets.

But the lipstick? It says here you can buy it for $17. A small price to pay for looking like you just stepped out of a Sargent painting. Or a *Vogue* cover.

Editors in cahoots with advertisers are nothing new. Women's magazines have a long history of sucking up to deep-pocketed clients.

Today's magazines originated as advertising circulars in Restoration London. By the 1760s, the modern editorial mix was already in place. Except that, for the next century or so, magazines had to make their profits from high cover prices.

Early American publishers proved a particularly pragmatic bunch. When the newly independent journalists were running low on material, they exercised Yankee ingenuity and pirated more from across the pond. When they were criticized for publishing so much circulation-building sentimental fiction, they reslugged the fiction as fact. (What preacher dared naysay life's lessons?) And, as the Regency libertine gave way to the Victorian domestic goddess and the scope of acceptable feminine ambition narrowed accordingly, they produced the first American fashion magazines: *Godey's Lady's Book* in 1830 and *Peterson's Magazine* in 1842.

Occasionally, they even allowed women to work on women's magazines, provided they were cheaper and better than any available males. (Not until John Mack Carter left *Good Housekeeping* in 1994 were all the editors of major women's magazines actually women.) Widowed mother of five Sarah Hale came to her job at *Godey's* with a track record that included authorship of classics such as "Mary Had a Little Lamb," and built the magazine to a pre-Civil War circulation of 150,000 despite prohibitive per-issue prices and postal costs. She still never earned as much as a man.

Post–Civil War improvements in transportation, printing, and postal service provided all kinds of windfalls for the magazine industry. Dozens of the women's titles started that would stay around for a while: *Good Housekeeping*, *Harper's Bazar* (the extra *a* arrived in 1929), *Ladies' Home Journal*, *McCall's*, and *Vogue*. Circulations soared.

Greedy for even more readers, *Ladies' Home Journal* publisher Cyrus Curtis slashed cover prices, gambling that he could recoup revenue by charging the advertisers more to reach a bigger audience. It worked. His competition cut cover prices too, and circulations began passing the million mark. From then on, advertising became the financial mainstay of most magazines.

When Condé Nast bought *Vogue* in 1909, he knew its tiny circulation wasn't much of a magnet. So he snared advertisers with snobbism, later exalted as "target marketing." Nast promised class instead of mass. Anyone who mattered read *Vogue*. If a potential advertiser didn't fall for that argument, Nast made it well understood that anyone who spent enough on ads was well treated on *Vogue* editorial pages too.

For the budding beauty industry, *Vogue* institutionalized the practice with "On Her Dressing Table," a column that seemed designed as a dumping ground for mentions too difficult to work into the rest of the magazine. By the 1920s, its authors had already perfected the skeptical-yet-snooty tone beauty editors have been using ever since: "Let us emphasize the fact that these are greaseless preparations—and that doesn't mean they are heavy or dense or drying. Quite the contrary. It means that they can't clog the pores."

Nast's approach became industry standard. Soon, though, beauty advertisers became too numerous to knock off in a single column, leading to the evolution of the practice called "editorial consideration." A company bought space and, in return, became part of the beauty editor's beat. Not quite quid pro quo, but the next best thing.

When it came time to put product credits on a cover or a big beauty feature, the editor sent pictures to whatever company she planned to favor with the credit. The company sent back a list of products to put in the caption. If, in its zeal to promote a certain color story, the company named products that looked nothing like the makeup in the pictures, it didn't matter. Readers rarely complained.

Big credits went to big advertisers. That explained why companies like Cover Girl and Clinique could get so many covers when their products were practically absent from professional makeup artists' kits. It also explained implausible attributions, like the time *Vanity Fair's* cover credit read that the makeup artist had used Chanel—even though the makeup artist for that particular cover happened to be Jeanine Lobell, the owner and founder of Stila.

A few covers still come out that way. The rest stopped in the 1990s when editors discovered they could save themselves trouble and placate even more advertisers by mentioning multiple companies. At the same time, computer retouching became so prevalent that accurate captions could be more misleading than inaccurate ones.

But the evolved system of "support" and "coverage" continues, because it benefits both parties. Ads are expensive. A single page in *Family Circle* costs $95,500. *Glamour* goes for over $74,000. *Vogue* over $61,000. *Allure* and *Elle* and *InStyle* at least $40,000. Adding a scent strip or running the ad on the back cover up those prices another 10 or 20 percent. Adding a product sample doubles or triples the cost.

Magazines need the money.

Atmosphere makes or breaks this kind of story. A *Family Circle* background has to look somewhat believable, hip yet homey. The magazine picked this studio because it has big, old-fashioned, casement windows that flood the space with natural sunshine. Normally, anyway. At the moment, the skies are Gothically gloomy and those big windows are curtained by sheets of rain.

While the photographer and his assistant rig a spotlight to fake sunshine, Linda worries her way down a checklist. Tomorrow, the weather's supposed to be sunny, which means that whatever she shoots now won't match whatever she shoots then. There's no time or budget to reshoot. And this is one magazine that doesn't really retouch. "We'll take out a nipple that's showing, but that's about it," she says, and then she makes that same sighing sound she made before the model casting.

Trying to get things off to a better start, Linda decides to go with a sure thing for the first shot: a blue-eyed blonde with one of those figures that looks good in anything.

Except that, this morning, nothing looks good. Three-quarter-length sleeves make the model look like a gawky kid outgrowing her clothes. Cuffed pants are too long. The funnel-neck top looks like a neck brace. The magenta top is too bright. But burgundy is too dark. And lavender is too light.

A shiny white shirt seems promising until Linda overhears an assistant call it "pretty—in a *Star Wars* kind of way."

While the model goes back to try something else, Linda signs for a FedEx package that's supposed to be full of fall jewelry. Instead, sparkly Christmas trees and rhinestone snowflakes spill out. Linda doesn't say a word. This time, looking like a puppy who's been kicked, she doesn't even sigh.

She pulls out her checklist and starts revising. She stares outside, amazed anew at the amounts of precipitation pouring down. Now the sighing starts up again.

The photographer and assistant use the time to fiddle with lights. Another half dozen people, inured to the hurry-up-and-wait pace of shoots, hang out, flip through magazines, pick at breakfast buffet leftovers, dish about who got what plastic surgery, and talk about travel plans.

The hair stylist is headed to Las Vegas "although I hate gambling. I always wish I'd gotten shoes instead."

Everybody's worked in California wine country. Ho hum. Miami Beach. Paris. Yawn. Tuscany too.

Crews work these shoots as a loss leader. Photographers work for a lower rate than they get for commercial jobs. Hair and makeup people work for a day rate that rarely tops $250 and can go as low as $135. Models make the same. Nobody gets rich doing editorials, but the job has its compensations.

"Ibiza? I've been there *so-o-o* much," whines one of today's freelancers. "But . . ." Pause. Audible intake of breath. "I may take off again."

"What about September? That's when I'll probably go this year."

Linda, who only travels to resorts she can feature in *Family Circle*, is too preoccupied to compare notes. She contemplates the blonde, now in rose. This isn't right either. She makes the little sighing sound. All this stuff looked fantastic on the hangers. She sends the blonde back to the racks for another try.

Jumping ahead on her list, Linda puts a brunette in a mohair-blend sweater for a fashion shot. The sweater sheds all over the studio, but at least that can be fixed. Off camera, an assistant hovers over the model with a lint roller, madly swiping mohair as it molts all over everything. On camera, the model reclines on her velvet chaise, the picture of calm and coziness.

During the twenty minutes that takes, they've found the blonde something to wear. But now her makeup needs freshening; more hurry up and wait. Standing at the makeup table, Linda makes more notes to herself, adds more chores to the checklist. Her next worry is what makeup products to put on the page next to the model's picture.

That won't be an easy one either. Linda can't write the kind of fiction featured on last night's investigative TV report. The sighing sounds are back. Integrity is just great, but it won't win her any prizes with the people she covers.

Fifteen minutes more and the blonde is back wearing the same pretty plum and berry colors that she started with this morning. Only she's not wearing enough of them. When the photographer takes his Polaroid, she doesn't look like she's wearing any makeup at all. So it's more eye shadow. More blush. More gloss. Another Polaroid.

Now the model's eyes look too blue. More eye shadow.

The next Polaroid shows the blonde wearing the same middle-of-the-road makeup featured in *Family Circle* for the last decade. Perfect.

The photographer starts shooting. At his shoulder, the makeup artist stands primed with powder, puff, and brushes, swooping in during film changes to dull down a shiny nose or shine up dull lips.

Twenty minutes and a half dozen touch-ups later, the first beauty picture is finished. The model looks like she's been caught off guard. Her hair seems slightly mussed, her makeup improvised.

Surely any reader could master this in a minute or two. Everything looks so effortless.

All the magazines are writing their fall stories by now. All of them working from the same press releases and products. All of them busy writing coverlines for issues that will thud into mailboxes, thick as telephone books for a fair-sized city. On the outside, all the stories sound alike. "Fall: The New Essentials." "24 Fall Makeup Must-Haves." "207 Looks You'll Love." On the inside, each is specific as a daydream.

Inside *W*, women exist in a world unconstrained by budget, weight gain, or what to wear to work. Pale-cheeked maidens photographed in arty poems of light and shadow are captioned with a beauty tip about blusher. Sleeping beauties recline on desert rocks while huge, hairy spiders are used to counterpoint the crispness of this season's white shirts.

In *Seventeen*, adolescence is the life stage of limitless possibility, populated by skinny, smiling girls with straight teeth and perfect skin. Adaptations of the latest runway looks, complete with product pointers and shopping tips, fill the beauty pages.

In *Harper's Bazaar*, putting on a new persona is as painless as buying new beauty products. The proof is in the lead beauty feature, where witty modulations of makeup and accessories make Kate Moss practically unrecognizable from one picture to the next. The headline says it all: "Change your lipstick, change your life."

What's new? Who would I like to be this season? What would I like to wear? Pick your story.

Linda has just signed off on the page proofs of her big fall feature. Pretty soon five or six million copies of her pronouncements will be rolling off the printer, bound for the supermarkets and mailboxes of America.

Her story, "What We Love for Fall," is relentlessly upbeat. In the *Family Circle* version of the season, quilting isn't a design quirk, it's "a boon for balancing out uneven figures." Impractical, teensy handbags are "adorable." Bruise-colored makeup is lyrically limned as "gunmetal" and "soft violet." And, if you can't afford the kind of thick cashmere that sets you back upwards of a thousand dollars per sweater, then Linda's molting mohair-blend offers "the same super softness."

Linda's pages include runway shots because her readers just love the runway. She's also crammed in beauty pictures, an illustrated time line, and cheery reassurances that work in all the buzzwords: "Being stylish is *easier than ever*, because what's hot this season is not only *beautiful*, but *wearable*."

She's even managed to picture a few beauty products that squeaked in under deadline—including Revlon's Thunder lipstick. According to her, the gray actually looks a little lavender in the right light. Really, it's not so bad. "It's a great way for my reader to get the feeling of gray, without looking too young," says Linda, who has long since learned to field whatever the industry pitches. Published in a context of chicken recipes and money-saving coupons, Revlon's fashion-forward lipstick reads as a fun fall splurge.

This season, let the beauty companies offer weird gray lipsticks. On the pages of *Family Circle*, the story that is fall makeup will be wearable, beautiful, and easier than ever.

July

SALES TRAINING: THE PARABLE
OF THE PINK CADILLAC

Pink Cadillacs! Diamond jewelry! Dream vacations!

The air around here positively glitters with exclamation points. "It's Your Turn!" promises the enormous banner over the entry to the enormous Dallas Convention Center. Parked nearby, where nobody can possibly miss it, a pearly pink Cadillac De Ville gleams its own promises under the unclouded Texas sun.

Everywhere else, the beauty industry is gearing up for its big selling season. In the flat, unforgiving heat of late July, Aerin's airy fantasy of "Winter Beach" is finally finding its way to store shelves. In one hundred Nordstroms across the country, beauty advisors are watching fall fashions and listening to fall color stories until they can recite them in their sleep. In the magazines, Revlon's ads are running right next to runway photos that completely contradict them.

Here in Dallas, they're gearing up for bigger and better things. Thirty-five thousand of the faithful are gathering for "Seminar," the storied annual convention of Mary Kay Cosmetics. Seminar's high drama draws so many devotees that, for years now, the company has had to hold five identical, separate Seminars—Sapphire, Ruby, Emerald, Pearl, and Diamond—and run them back-to-back just to fit everybody in.

This summer, like every summer since 1964, buckets of tears will be shed. Grown women will dress up in gowns and crowns and weep in exultation at winning new cars and 14-karat jewelry and trips to far-off lands. They will exchange sales strategies and sob some more as they share struggles in sisterhood. And, when the whole thing is over, they will head home dry-eyed and determined, positive that beauty is one of the best things to ever happen to women.

Right now, as the industry hunkers down for the big one-two punch of fall-holiday, every company has some sort of pep rally or product training in progress. But no other company tells its story on such epic scale. At Mary Kay, the romance between women and beauty products is a quasi-religious quest, full of foes vanquished and dragons slain. As told here in Texas, it turns into the best kind of love story: It's got one powerful Fairy Godmother, skips the Prince Charming part, and promises every good girl will live happily ever after.

This woman has gone through hell—absolute hell!—to get to Dallas. She left the husband and kids in Fresno at the crack of dawn this morning. Flew to L.A., got rerouted to Chicago, ended up in Denver, then spent hours there. "Would have been easier to go back home," she tells the SuperShuttle driver as she hands him her Mary Kay discount coupon. She's completely missed Day Zero, which means she's missed the factory tour and the Mary Kay museum. And, by the time she gets to her hotel, she'll have missed dinner with her director and the rest of her group.

Legions of Mary Kay ladies in red jackets have been arriving all day, the driver tells her. They've been overrunning the airport all week. Either headed to Seminar or headed home. Seems like every last one of them has tried to sell him lotion or aftershave or something for his wife, he adds, throwing her a don't-go-there glance in the rearview mirror.

Stopped before she can get out her sales pitch, the woman sinks back against the seat, looking a little relieved. At any rate, she's happy to be here at last. She allows as how she's far from the only one who had a rough time: "My director has cancer and just got out of the hospital. When she goes home she has to start chemo—didn't want to start chemo now and be sick for Seminar!"

. . .

Day One of Diamond, the last Seminar in this year's se-
ries. At 8:30 sharp, more than seven thousand Mary Kay
representatives are in their assigned places. White
women. Black women. Latina women. Two or three
heavily pregnant women. A delegation of tiny, lost-
looking women from Thailand. Proudly plus-sized
women. Women as young as their twenties, like the law
student who works full-time, goes to school full-time,
and still sells prize-winning amounts of product on the
side. Hearing-impaired women. Legally blind women.
Row after row of women in wheelchairs. Thousands of
baby-boomers with perky expressions and sensible hairdos. Plus a few husbands scattered through the audience
like accessories.

Nary a frump in the bunch. Not a single bare face.
Despite the lamented lack of Mary Kay–brand hair-
spray, not one hair out of place in the entire arena. De-
fying today's 101-degree weather, every single soul
wears recommended Seminar attire right down to the
pantyhose and pumps, each skirt and blouse and blazer
as crisp as if she just stepped out of a bandbox. The notorious red jacket is everywhere, a signal that the
woman wearing it has gathered at least three others into
the Mary Kay fold.

Not that anyone stops at the basics. Over and above
that recommended attire, each woman has turned herself into a walking advertisement of her own sales

prowess. Most Mary Kay regalia is made of rhinestones and most women are covered with it. Rhinestone ladders reach to rhinestone stars. Rhinestone numbers write sales figures. Rhinestone letters spell slogans. And where there are no possibilities for pins, the women hang ribbons. Ribbons unfurl from nametags. Ribbon rosettes, the kind pinned to winning horses, flutter from sleeves because there's no place left to put them on the jacket fronts.

Each woman has paid $165, plus her own transportation, food, and lodging, to get here. No one will leave disappointed. Slick as a Miss America pageant, Seminar is staged the way its audience is dressed. This morning, the professional chorus line belts out "It's not where you start, it's where you finish!" with the dead-on precision of a drill team. Company execs read tales of triumph from teleprompters with the poise of professional newscasters. Company oaths are projected on huge video screens and smoothly subtitled in Spanish so everyone can swear along. Award winners are rehearsed to acknowledge their cheering sisters with a palm-out, stiff-armed wave that would do any beauty queen proud. Like sheepdogs in tuxedos, silent, self-effacing men escort the ladies on and off stage, moving the women smoothly in and out of their moment in the spotlight.

Each edition of Seminar follows the same ritual. Mary Kay Ash, the company's founder, liked to kick things off by reading a sentimental song. (To this day, nobody has been able to milk the line "I believe for every drop of rain that falls, a flower grows" quite like Mary Kay.) So today, to honor the founder's own earnestness, the speaker intones the old Diana Ross hit "It's My Turn" with many, many meaningful pauses. By the time she gets to " . . . it's my turn to start for number one," thousands of jaws are clenched with determination.

After that, the audience is primed. Mary Kay ladies love hard-luck stories, and Seminar's got more of them than the old *Queen for a Day* show. First comes the inspirational tale of a consultant who managed to meet sales goals despite her son's move, her own elective surgery, her subsequent sprained ankle, and her mother-in-law's death. Big score on the Clap-O-Meter.

Next up, that paragon of perseverance: Abraham Lincoln, who, for reasons unquestioned by the audience, is described as "the greatest Ivy League president in our history." Lincoln's life is a positive black pit of bad luck. "Wooh!" go the ladies, every time he suffers another setback. "Wooh!" they say when they hear about his six-month nervous breakdown. But when the speaker comes to her punchline—"elected president"— arms fly upward, fists pump the air, and mad clapping resounds. The moral of the story: "If he listened with his ears, he would have been discouraged." That gets a standing ovation.

Mary Kay's own tale is, of course, a triumph against the odds, and no one is allowed to forget it for a minute. Although this audience could recite it like a favorite Bible story, that doesn't stop it from being lovingly retold again and again. How Mary Kay was born in Hot Wells, Texas, in a year that's reluctantly and disingenuously given as 1918 but was probably 1915. How little Mary Kay's father was stricken with tuberculosis. How Mary Kay's mother, Lula, unable to earn the same wage as a man, worked fourteen hours a day, seven days a week, leaving little Mary Kay to care for her daddy and herself. "You can do it, Mary Kay!" her mother would urge over the telephone as she talked the child through chores. "You can do it!" How Mary Kay cooked meals and bought her own clothes at the tender age of seven. How she married at the tender age of seventeen.

When the story picks up again, Mary Kay is a single mom with three kids to support. She moves to Dallas to toil for a direct sales company. Mary Kay outsells, out-earns, outproduces just about everybody. She's good. Better than the men. Year after year she expands territory and sets records until, in the early 1960s, a man—a man she trained herself!—is made her supervisor and given twice her salary. Deciding that the old boy network has done her dirt one too many times, she quits.

Remarried, Mary Kay retires for a month, then comes back with a vengeance. As men are wont to do, her husband dies at the most inconvenient time, just as she is about to launch a brand-new company. She stays on schedule anyway. Mary Kay Cosmetics opens for business on Friday the 13th of September, 1963.

From that first day, Mary Kay pledges that her company will empower her fellow females, a sacred pledge endowing her with superhuman strength. The heroine's weapon is humble stuff—cosmetics—scorned by those of lesser knowledge and weaker spirit. Yet her own belief is so strong that she triumphs against all odds. Her rewards are a multinational kingdom, a nineteen-thousand-square-foot pink palace in north Dallas, and coffers overflowing with glittering gems.

In the best tradition of beauty entrepreneurs like Madame, Miss Arden, and Estée, Mary Kay is short, busty, and blessed with a good complexion. She wears her blond hair big. She wears her makeup heavy. She crams closets full of fantasies of femininity. Feather boas. Sequinned minks. Pink gowns piled with paillettes and passementerie. She puts in sixteen-hour days, but prides herself on always looking as though she just stepped out of a beauty parlor. She earns like a man, but no one can ever accuse her of looking or acting less than feminine.

And no matter how rich and successful she gets, Mary Kay never forswears her sacred pledge. In Mary Kay's company, every woman starts out the same way: as a beauty consultant who antes up for her demonstration showcase, pays regulation wholesale prices for the products, and conducts the same kind of skin care classes. The consultant gets no salary, no vacation, no health benefits. But she makes $5 on every $10 lipstick she can sell.

How far she advances depends on how much she sells. So do her earnings. No man is promoted over her or paid more money for the same job.

According to legend, door-to-door Bible salesman David H. McConnell unwittingly discovered a gold mine when he started giving away perfume samples with his wares. Noticing that fine, God-fearing Christian women preferred beauty products to Bibles, he switched to full-time beauty sales, and founded the California Perfume Company, later and better known as Avon, in 1886.

His second stroke of luck came when he recruited a ball of fire known as Mrs. P. F. E. Albee to do the selling. McConnell had enough sense to stay in New York and let Mrs. Albee hit the road. He stayed put, managed things in Manhattan, built the factory in Suffern, and taught Sunday school, letting his salesladies recruit more salesladies who were eager to get out of the house or off the farm and earn some money of their own. By 1900, Avon ladies—albeit not yet known by that name—were an American institution.

McConnell's success was one of many. Today, direct-sales companies like Avon and Mary Kay account for about a fifth of the beauty products sold in the United States. One hundred years ago, they were often the only game in town.

Unless she lived in a big city, a woman either bought

cosmetics from a door-to-door salesman, made her own, or did without. (Although the Sears catalogue carried beauty products as early as the 1890s, parcel post wouldn't arrive until 1913, so even mail-order meant a trip to the nearest post office.) And cosmetics, which still had a shady reputation, never sold as well when some city slicker was vending them. Sales came easier when that nice lady who lived down the road was doing the peddling.

For a customer, the saleslady's visit was a nice break. She could stop for a chat, play with pretty colors; feel, for a few minutes, like she was one of those spoiled city women who went to a salon every week to have someone smile at her and dress her hair and tend to her complexion.

For a saleslady, even going door to door on cold calls was a big improvement over the drudgery of a factory or farm. In Mrs. Albee's day, when "working woman" meant manual laborer, selling was one of the few things a woman without special training could do. Selling beauty was the one thing she could do better than a man.

Like Helena Rubinstein, Elizabeth Arden, Estée Lauder, and dozens of beauty entrepreneurs before her, Mary Kay used skin care as her hook. Unlike them, she didn't start with some snooty, highfalutin', European formula. She built her business on recipes brewed up by an Arkansas tanner, who'd been inspired to concoct cosmetics when he noticed how much softer and smoother his hands looked after a day curing deer hides. Mary Kay gave his family $500 for a copy of the formulas and spread the word.

Then, as now, first-timers were invited for a free facial using Mary Kay products. Unlike the Avon lady, the Mary Kay consultant didn't go to a customer's home, the customer came to her. So did four or five other prospects. (Mary Kay prices also ran roughly double Avon's, meaning that a single sale scored twice the revenue.) Following a format every housewife already knew from Tupperware parties, the beauty get-together was nice and social, and the consultant could sell half a dozen women in the same time it took to sell one. If that first session didn't snag them, a free follow-up session usually did.

Since 1963, enough customers have gotten snagged to put Mary Kay's corporation in the number two spot for direct sales of cosmetics. Avon still leads with three million representatives spread over 137 countries and $5.3 billion in revenue (plus its claim to be the world's largest publisher, by virtue of its biweekly brochures). But Mary Kay is right behind, with half a million consultants in thirty-three countries racking up $1.1 billion at wholesale.

What's more, business practices once peculiar to Mary Kay are cropping up at other companies. Dallas-based BeautiControl, number three in direct sales with

$130 million, uses the same sales structure, has practically the same prices, throws a Seminar-style "Celebration" each year, and lends Cadillacs or Mercedes to top salesladies. BeautiControl's owners even built an eighteen-thousand-square-foot fake French chateau in Mary Kay's old neighborhood, then joined the same Baptist church.

At Avon last year, sixty-five hundred representatives paid their own way to a two-and-a-half-day, Seminar-style national convention in Orlando. Next week, ten thousand are expected to attend the second convention, which Avon promises to make an annual event.

Meanwhile, Mary Kay shamelessly touts itself as "the best-selling brand of skin care and color cosmetics in the U.S."—a claim that it bases on "most recently published sales data," although most industry rankings put Revlon or Avon millions ahead of it. However, as the Founder herself once put it: "When you have confidence in yourself, you'll create a positive buying environment." Mary Kay knew it pays to put a pretty face on things.

"The Lord sent it into my life!" testifies Ruth Williams-McCance. Back in 1968, Ruth started with Mary Kay as a part-time job—in addition to the full-time job she was already working to put her husband through dental school and support their four kids, the youngest of whom was eight months old.

When it came time to pay for her first big order, she had to take out a small loan, which meant waiting for her husband to get out of class and accompany her to the bank because, breadwinner or no, "A woman couldn't borrow money in those days—especially not in Texas." When that same husband walked out nine years later, leaving her with herself, four children, and a grandchild to support on $300 a month, she kept the family going with Mary Kay earnings.

Now, all these years later, Ruth is a financially secure, happily remarried executive senior sales director. She is fluent in Spanish, a skill acquired opening Mary Kay territory in Mexico. She owns and flies her own plane, which is painted pink. The plane's call letters, N240MK, are the number of her Mary Kay unit.

In the Mary Kay strongholds of the South and Midwest, generations of women have grown up on lore like this. From the cradle, they hear parables of gumption set in and around the beauty industry. The makeover that lifted a woman's spirits when she felt low. The plain girl who persevered until she became a beauty queen. The single mom who put her kids through college on makeup sales margins. Early on, they learn that you can't always count on men in this life. But beauty can heal your heartache and make you some money besides.

Forget feminism. There's nothing like making money off other women to prove how powerful sisterhood can be. When one consultant recruits others, she gets a commission on everything they sell. If her recruits go out and do the same, then she gets a commission on what the second generation sells too. And so it goes, as each woman gets pushed higher and higher up the pyramid by the women who come after her.

That kind of sales scheme has been around forever. But it was the beauty business that managed to turn "multilevel sales" into a way of making all those girlhood fairy-story fantasies come true. Mary Kay crowned top sellers with tiaras, told them they were beautiful inside and out, and praised them to the skies. Like a glittering, flossy-haired godmother, she bestowed "Cinderella gifts," so-called because they represented indulgences her ladies would never allow themselves. Fur coats. Flashy cars. Fine jewelry. She even tailored her Cinderella gifts to the territory: In Taiwan, the pink Cadillac turns into a pink Toyota. In Germany, it becomes a pink Mercedes.

As the women she called her "daughters" plugged their way to the top of the pyramid, Mary Kay was right behind them, telling them "You can do it!" the way her mama had told her. No one could sell salespeople better. How she'd inspire 'em! Take 'em on personal tours of her pink mansion. Feed 'em her very own home-baked cookies. Fire 'em up with pep talks that turned timid country bumpkins into supersellers powering pink Caddies.

When she entered Seminar, wearing the spectacularly sparkly gowns now in the vitrines of the Mary Kay museum, she did everything but descend from a cloud. Looking like the missing link between Mae West and Dolly Parton, the Founder would disembark from a horse-drawn carriage. Or a hot-air balloon. Or a whirling merry-go-round. Those Seminar appearances ended, alas, after her stroke in 1996; thereafter, like the aged Estée Lauder, she was never seen in public, and the members of her company reverentially referred to her in the past tense.

Her presence remains inescapable though. Before her stroke, the company shot enough tape of Mary Kay to keep the cult of personality going for at least another decade. She hovers over these proceedings via audio and video, in anecdote and aphorism. The faithful call her mottos "Mary Kay-isms" and cite them the way a preacher cites holy writ.

"There are two rules to success. Number one: Get started. Number two: Don't quit."

"When you come to the end of your rope, tie a knot and hang on!"

"What do you have that you can't have fixed?"

"Fail forward to success."

And the most famous, the company motto, the ultimate Mary Kay-ism: "God first, family second, and career third."

God, family, Mary Kay . . . sometimes they get all mixed up. In the vocabulary of revelation and the syntax of redemption, a morning speaker intones: "In Mary Kay there are many gifts, and one of the gifts that we receive in Mary Kay is Seminar." Another paraclete comes to the podium with a teaching from the Founder that begins "It is far better to dare mighty things, to win glorious triumphs. . . ."

"God is using our company as a vehicle to help women become the beautiful creatures that He created," Mary Kay reminds the assembly via tape. Star recruiters are sworn in with an oath that begins "I pledge to live true to the Golden Rule philosophy." Consultants are entreated to "carry the torch." Sales groups are praised for being "pure of heart."

Mid-morning, an African American sales director takes the stage to lead a gospel-style call-and-response. "Diamonds do dominate!" she hollers. Thousands of true believers holler back.

Clapping and swaying, she gets the congregation on its feet. Behind her on stage, a kick line of Mary Kay ladies clap and sway along. As she sings out the many benefits of working for Mary Kay, she enacts each one. She pretends she's behind the wheel of a huge Cadillac. The audience pretends too, ecstatically sticking their arms into the empty air in front of them.

A Mary Kay–inspired macarena comes next. Ribbons wave merrily from blazers as the ladies shimmy without stepping out of their places. The scattering of husbands look sheepish, but gallantly try to get in the groove. "Wooh!" thousands of women scream.

"Are you ready to raise your expectation?" calls the leader. She pumps both arms overhead. Thousands of women shout back "Let's raise it!" and push at the sky.

During lunch break, consultants cluster in little groups, sipping Diet Cokes through straws to protect their lipstick, nibbling popcorn kernels pinched prudently between the pads of thumb and index finger to preserve their manicures, or joining the very long, very slow lines to the ladies' rooms.

Consultants visit the "Driven by the Dream" display and ogle the company cars. All of them free—free!—to any consultant who meets quota. (And all of them whisked away as fast as Cinderella's coach when sales fall.) In the Expo area, insurance reps sell "product protection" for makeup damaged by fire, flood, or other acts of God.

On the cement steps outside Area C, a half-dozen smokers try to find a spot out of the relentless sunshine. Like everybody else here, they trade tales of triumphs over the odds. A Red Jacket repeats a story featuring the Founder to a Seminar first-timer who's somehow managed to miss it.

It seems that there once was a consultant whose husband had been given only a few months to live. Mary Kay, who'd lost a favorite husband to cancer in 1980, heard about the situation and flew him to Dallas, where he was examined by a specialist who also happened to be a recipient of Mary Kay's research grants. Miraculously, the specialist's treatment sent the cancer into remission. Whereupon the consultant spread her wares on her husband's hospital bed and sold Mary Kay products to the attending nurses.

The women sitting on the stairs drag deeply on their cigarettes and nod their bouffant heads in an unspoken amen.

Back inside, the arena darkens, lights flash, actors posing as paparazzi swarm the stage, and a rapt audience watches "Lessons and Legends," a video biography of Mary Kay. Made-up to the nines, crowned with her cotton-candy wig, decked with diamond jewelry, Mary Kay goes toe-to-toe with Morley Safer in excerpts from an old *60 Minutes* profile. Morley looks abashed by her clever answers. Mary Kay wins the encounter hands down. Especially in this edit.

From there, it's straight into more speeches and sales recognition awards. Women stare at the stage as if it were a vision of Canaan. A song and dance number called "Too Hot to Stop" recognizes winners of something called a Red Jacket Rally. The music goes on and on and on as hundreds of women parade across the stage. Each one beams like this is the best thing that's ever happened to her. One wears a fireman's hat to show she's too hot to stop.

Midafternoon, husbands are dispatched to classes on

how to help their wives achieve success, and Seminar gets down to girly stuff like new products. It's the first mention of makeup today.

Makeup is means to an end for this crowd, and on-stage descriptions give no evidence of aesthetic agonies endured à la Estée Lauder and Revlon. In direct sales, a color story doesn't have to attract anybody to a counter. It just has to be pretty and look a little different from the last one. Within a few minutes they've wrapped up fall, a collection of russets and plums that looks like a more vivid version of Avon's color story. Then, from fall, it's straight to a $40 Filofax-sized makeup kit called the Color Storybook, which looks exactly like the kits Trish McEvoy and Bobbi Brown and Philosophy have been making for years. One speaker suggests using it to start a "Mary Kay Book Club."

Once that's over with, it's time for the treat: a fashion show from Nordstrom. These ladies love fashion. Thousands have added flowery scarves or big earrings or other accessories to their official attire. They can't wait to see what's "in" for fall.

"Fall is very streamlined, very sophisticated. But most of all it is subtle," the ladies covered in rhinestone pins and horse-show ribbons soon learn. As the fashion commentator explains that fall's number one silhouette is slim and vertical, murmurs of "My, those models are skinny!" ripple around the arena. There's an awful lot of gray onstage. Prodded by the commentator, the ladies applaud politely. Finally, during the evening wear segment, a size-14 model sashays centerstage gauded in glorious shining gold from head to toe. "Wooh!" Real fashion at last. "Wooh!" Unprompted pandemonium breaks out as the ladies hoot approval.

On that upbeat note, a few more new products are announced and cheered before the session adjourns. "This is such a motivator" gushes one consultant as everyone heads back to her hotel to get ready for tonight's goings on. As they file out beneath the banners promising "It's Your Turn!" seven thousand women glow with the guiding light of the freshly inspired.

Mary Kay was far from the first to sell beauty as balm in Gilead. In the early 1900s, two self-made, African American magnates, Annie Turnbo, founder of Poro hair care, and Sarah Breedlove, founder of the Madam C. J. Walker company, established hugely profitable national networks by lavishing top saleswomen with the same kind of perks and public acclamation. Their strongholds were also the South and Midwest, where women one generation away from slavery could be their own boss—and win diamond jewelry!—just by selling beauty products.

Both women made beauty sound like the noblest of callings: Become part of a business predicated on charity, the Golden Rule, and acts of Godliness. Sell a bottle of Wonderful Hair Grower and strike a blow for race and gender equality. Join the many fine, God-fearing women who made good livings from beauty—women who would otherwise be slaving for subsistence wages from white people.

Both businesses bore bountiful witness to wonders beauty hath wrought. No tycoon, before or since, could top Madam C. J. Walker as a rags-to-riches story. Born to newly emancipated sharecroppers on a Louisiana cotton plantation in 1867, Sarah Breedlove was the first in her family not slave born. Her career as a freelance washerwoman commenced at age seven, after both parents died of overwork and malnutrition, abetted by a bout of yellow fever. At age fourteen, she married an itinerant laborer. By seventeen, she was a mother. By nineteen, she was a widowed single mother.

Sarah somehow learned to read and write, and did enough white people's dirty laundry to send her own daughter to college. Living in St. Louis, the headquarters of Annie Turnbo, she had a chance to suss out Poro's operation and briefly did a selling stint herself— over and above her laundry business. She noticed that Poro's appeal to racial pride didn't do business any harm. At thirty-seven, she kissed three decades of wash-tubs, lye soap, and steaming irons good-bye and started selling her own hair products door to door in Denver.

A St. Louis ad salesman named C. J. Walker was impressed enough with her business acumen to follow her to Denver, marry her, and help her start a mail-order business. By the end of its first year, that business was bringing in $10 a week. Her husband thought that was great. Sarah thought she could do better, so she hit the road on an eighteen-month sales trip. By herself. The marriage didn't work out, but Sarah continued to use his name and C. J. remained a certified representative of her company until the day he died.

Sarah hit the road so hard that, a dozen years later, she'd practically made herself into a millionaire. *The New York Times*, a paper for white people, ran a picture feature on her thirty-four-room mansion in the ritzy New York suburb of Irvington, an estate that included a sunken Italian garden, swimming pool, gold-trimmed piano, and fancy pipe organ. The *Times* also reported, in its best man-bites-dog manner, that the house was designed by a Negro architect.

Less than two years later, at age fifty-one, Sarah was dead from overwork, hastened by high blood pressure. Despite doctor's orders, she never slowed down or stopped the selling trips. Finally confined to bed in her fancy mansion, she gasped out, "I want to live to help my race." Those were her last words.

To the very end, she preached "Women's Duty to Women." She exhorted her representatives with mottos, anecdotes, and aphorisms based on her own success. She could do it. So could they. She'd say, "Don't sit down and wait for the opportunities to come. Get up and make them!"

Compared to the alternatives, selling beauty was a good job for a woman.

· · ·

"I thought I'd surely died and went to heaven when I started working for Mary Kay," says Senior Director Bonnie Radke, age seventy-nine. "I could work short hours, come home rested." After decades with the company, Bonnie sounds freshly grateful for the sweet salvation of selling beauty products. "Mary Kay's done more to change women's lives than any woman in this century."

Before she joined up in 1967, Bonnie worked full-time in a factory, pressing men's pants. She'd started at a salary of twenty-five cents an hour, twenty-five years before. By switching to piecework, she doggedly turned herself into the factory's top earner, taking home $100 a day. "That's thousands and thousands of pants."

With her husband and two children, Bonnie lived on a cotton farm in Hillsboro, a town in the Texas hill country halfway between Waco and Dallas. One day a Mary Kay sales director came to town. Bonnie asked to be recruited. She'd been hoping to get a job in retail, or go into business for herself, "Because I wanted to make as much as a man."

The director never got around to recruiting Bonnie. So Bonnie went directly to Dallas and applied at company headquarters. Mary Kay, the Founder herself, became Bonnie's director. But even though "I got everything straight from the horse's mouth," Bonnie doesn't think that being trained by the Founder gave her any great advantage. "No. It was my own enthusiasm that made me successful."

Bonnie had always loved beauty; she'd been using skin care since she was eight years old. "I wanted to preserve my beautiful complexion," she explains, patting her weathered cheek as if it were still smooth as a baby's bottom. Every single day of those twenty-five years hunched over an industrial iron, she styled her blond hair and wore makeup to bring out the blue in her eyes. "I was dressed up like a movie star in that sweat factory, although inside of thirty minutes I'd be soaked through."

After quitting the factory job, it was no time at all before she was making one hundred dollars a day again. Bonnie didn't have much of a knack for booking facials or skin care classes, so she went back to the piecework strategy that had served her so well in the factory. She hustled "private specials." During the days, she drove a tractor in the cotton fields. Come sundown, she would sell and, when it got too late for that, she would do paperwork and scheme up new ways to build her unit.

Her husband thought Mary Kay was a waste of time. He wanted her to do nothing but drive a tractor for him. "He said, 'You'll never do it,'" she remembers. "I said, 'Stand back and watch me.'" He would shout, "You'll not make no money." He would threaten to throw her products out in the yard. Even after the big money started, even after she became a director in 1972, he never relented. He might brag to everybody else, but he never went with her to Seminar. When she won a trip to Hawaii, he wouldn't go. She took her daughter instead.

"He went to his grave thinking I was a threat to him," she says, still sounding thwarted. "My husband was negative about Mary Kay till the day he died."

Twenty-seven years later, Bonnie remembers that day too well. "He didn't believe in insurance." So, when her husband suffered a stroke and a heart attack, it cost her $5,000 a day for intensive care and another $5,000 to bury him. By that time, she could afford it. She was well on her way with Mary Kay. She hired help and kept working the farm. She educated her two children. Now she brags that she owns a brick house and "a half section of land" (320 acres). Her age-spotted hands are covered in shiny rings and she calls herself "a self-made millionaire."

Bonnie sometimes had $1,000 days with Mary Kay. Her sales topped $2,000 a month—sometimes going as high as $18,000—for 287 straight months. She attained the number one spot for sales in the entire company. She wore crowns. She entered the Queen's Court. "Once you go up on that stage, you'll want to be up there again." She won mink coats. She drove pink Cadillacs. She took trips. When Mary Kay announced a contest that would award a gold-plated goblet to anyone with a monthly wholesale of $1,000, Bonnie became queen of the golden goblets. "I had more gold than Fort Knox."

These days, Bonnie supervises about thirty women. She says she's seen a lot of women join up who are dedicated and work hard but don't stick to it, because their men didn't want them to be in Mary Kay. Bonnie understands all about that. But she stuck it out. She could do it. So could they.

When she tells her story, Bonnie's ardor is still genuine, her wrinkled face is full of unfeigned amazement. Even now, being free of the pants pressing, the tractor driving, and the drudgery seems too good to be true. "This? This is easy work."

September

AT THE COUNTERS:
ANOTHER HAPPY ENDING

ON A POSTCARD-PERFECT FRIDAY, when blue skies bless the Seattle suburbs and September sun sparkles off the bay, women crowd the Estée Lauder counter at Bellevue Square, transfixed by Aerin's fantasia of blustery weather and wintry beaches. Under fluorescent light inside a climate-controlled mall, they swipe lipsticks and happily dream of overcast skies and chilly days.

At the Dior counter, women on their way to the mall for a day's shopping stop to watch a video of Dior couture. As another poem of Proustian, Parisian excess appears on the monitor, a woman in a Gap sweatsuit cries out, "Now that's the *real* me!" as her friend in jeans and sneakers nods in heartfelt agreement.

Chanel's fall story was about Paris runways too, but

it's already sold out, much to the disappointment of the woman who stands here swearing, "I *only* wear Chanel!" M·A·C's story is the rock star look, underlined by the use of a young man as its model—a bit of transgender boldness completely lost on this customer, nostalgically buying because "This is perfect to wear for my anniversary tonight."

Ten months of industry dramas and dilemmas have come to this. Women stick their fingers into eye shadows, squirt their wrists with scent, page through the magazines on the counters, watch videos, and circle the department looking for more. The beauty business is having another banner season. No one seems to notice that fall stories change completely from one counter to the next. No one seems to care.

Why should they? Everywhere else, fall looks like a prison sentence. The bleak prophecies of last year's Première Vision hang like a pall. Up the escalator and all through the mall, racks fairly groan under the weight of that rigorous beauty and gorgeous gray. Shoppers drift by, riffle the racks, read the low numbers on the size labels and the high numbers on the price tags, and move on.

Down here, it's like a souk full of storytellers trying to outdo each other. Numbers are nowhere to be found. Chaos and color saturate air already reeking of Pleasures and Hypnotic Poison and Allure. A huge yellow Harley sits in front of Lancôme where, if you try a makeover today, the leathered-up beauty advisor will snap your picture as a bad-ass biker chick. "Go for it, Barb!" whoops one woman as her forty-something friend mounts the motorcycle. Across the aisle at Lauder, announcements painted on the floor guarantee that no one can miss the promotion—even if they walk by wearing blinders.

At Bobbi Brown, a makeup virgin shyly confesses, "No one's ever touched my face," to the disbelieving beauty advisor. "Oh, honey!" says the saleswoman, settling her gently into a makeover chair. "You are gonna love this!"

Regulars check out the department's remapped real estate. Guerlain is gone, replaced by a makeup-with-a-message line, which calls its nail polishes "Vibrational Remedies" and puts Saint-John's-wort in lipsticks. Origins has installed a three-and-a-half-foot-high gumball machine dispensing "sensory therapy": Pop in a quarter and buy Peace of Mind. Nearby, three women at another self-actualization counter debate which bath gel they like best: Pumpkin Pie or Chocolate Chip Cookie Dough? Eyes closed, they inhale deeply and frown in concentration.

Walk right up, get your free makeover, gawk at the New York and Paris runways, get a version of the near future with all the things you want and none of the things you don't. Check out the magazines. Hang out for an hour. Be a romantic heroine on a windswept, wintry beach, a couture client, a rock star, a bad-ass biker chick. Walk away less blue, less bored.

There's always something good going on in the beauty department.

Where and how and why the love affair is conducted may change, but its rules of attraction remain constant. A century ago, beauty companies were pushing products with the same kind of romantic stories, pretentious promotions, and inspired goofiness that are still working so well here at the mall.

In those days, though, women had to go to salons to find the kind of fulfillment they're getting over the counters this morning. No one really imagined the fantasy and frivolity of beauty sales would transfer to anyplace as public and prosaic as a department store. Even when Helena Rubinstein and Elizabeth Arden came along, neither was eager to put her precious products where she couldn't control their presentation. Anyway, business was good, expansion was as easy as opening another salon, and a little mail order filled in the blanks.

Then, as now, mark-up on beauty products started around 100 percent and went up from there—often to 1000 percent. Coveting a cut of that, department store suitors convinced the coy Madame and Miss Arden that their companies could earn enormous profit independent of the investment involved in owning additional salons. With that kind of free money in their crosshairs, both ladies were ready to try limited distribution.

The deals they won from the department stores ensured that beauty would never be sold in the same way as anything else. Let merchandise mix in other departments; at the beauty counter, brands would be forever segregated. Let the store uniform other employees; counters would be forever staffed by women whose dress and demeanor is decreed by the brand, and who would forever remain as beholden to the brand as the store. (For decades, most were direct employees, a system largely supplanted by "salary support," which means the beauty company augments the store paycheck.) Let the store run sales and specials in other departments, in beauty there would be no markdowns. Let standard store policy be damned.

To get things up and running, Miss Arden happily delegated supervision of store accounts to her first husband, who invented a doozie of a training and distribution system before she divorced him. Madame, who never did anything by halves, immersed herself in the new business up to her couture-clad elbows. Periodically, she would grab one of her numerous female relatives (usually her sister Manka) and take to the road with the vigor of a vaudevillian. She'd swoop into town early, boss around beauty advisors before the store opened, do personal consultations all day, break bread with local worthies, give interviews, then be back on the train and on to the next town. When distribution got too big for her to do the whistle-stop tours herself, Madame delegated them to her sister Manka. Then to her niece, Mala.

Standing at counters in Portland and St. Louis and Boston—and, later on, in some really Podunk places— she spouted story after story, each more far-fetched and fantastic than the next. The way Madame told it, kohl wasn't just some black stuff you taught a customer to apply around her eyes; it was the magic Cleopatra used to bewitch Caesar and Marc Antony. (When she really got going, it was also the magic that she personally invoked to make over Pola Negri and Theda Bara when her inspired eye goo turned them from shabby slatterns into silver screen vamps.) A visitor from another world, she would appear on the selling floor in her couture Balenciaga, Chanel, or Dior, accessorized with diamonds the size of desk lamps, wearing makeup that most women saw only on the stage.

Audiences ate it up. Housewives and secretaries would stand for hours to learn the new mode in Paris, the hot gossip from Hollywood, the latest doings of café society. It hardly mattered if any of it was true or not. Madame spoke of things that were strange and wondrous and then made you believe you could buy them at her counter. As the salons had been, beauty departments became a place where women went for entertainment and escapism.

Estée Lauder didn't do anything to change that. Her contribution would be adding a salon's sense of safe haven and special treatment to the most hectic, high-trafficked area of any department store.

Long before she could afford to advertise, Estée got

women to her counter with more makeovers, samples, gifts with purchase, and therapeutic doses of personal attention than they could get anywhere else. She believed in the laying on of hands: swooping through stores patting faces, squeezing elbows, and pressing flesh. When business got bigger, Estée kept it up. Which meant her competition did too. The beauty department became where you headed to be stroked, no matter what mood you were in, no matter how tough your day had been.

The exclusive became inclusive. The latest fashions, the wildest fantasies, the most ardent attentions were put front and center in every department store. Right where any woman could walk up and take advantage.

Maybe this isn't what she imagined when she promised to take the girls to the mall this afternoon. But now that she's here?

The mom in her mid-thirties and two teenage girls stand at the Dior counter, dazzled by the *défilé* on the video monitor. As the three of them watch, the clothes become ever more beaded and Beardsleyesque, ever more ornamented and overrefined. Each model as decadently attenuated as an Art Nouveau arabesque.

The fifteen-year-old finds this absolutely awesome, and says so to her mother. Her half-sister, too grown up to be so gushy, giggles. Mom grins without taking her eyes off the screen.

Yeah, this is it. This is what they don't have. "We're ready for our makeovers!" the mom calls out to the closest beauty advisor.

Whereupon the three encounter Donna Rae, Dior's other big attraction. Today Donna looks like the Cher of the 1970s. Her brows are plucked to pencil lines. Her nails are square and red. Her long brunette hair has blatant blond stripes. She wears tight toreador pants, a six-foot feather boa, a fake diamond the size of a fist, and the kind of makeup these three have never seen in broad daylight. Both teenagers stare, open-mouthed.

Mom goes first. She tilts her face up to Donna, trusting and relaxed. You know Donna is up on all the latest. All you have to do is look at her. Donna chatters away about her own makeup—"When you work in cosmetics, less is not enough"—as the two proceed through the preliminary skin care and foundation. Occasionally, the mom glances over at her fifteen-year-old, whose own session is under way in a chair directly opposite. The kid is having a great time too.

When it's time for the good stuff like colors and liners and mascaras, Donna speaks of "smokey eyes" and "adding intrigue" and "transformation" in feeling, florid language. While she listens to the spiel, mom can still see the monitor out of the corner of her eye. Even if she had one of those $50,000 dresses, she'd have no place to wear it. Makeup, though, that's different. Donna is showing her all kinds of tricks to using the eye shadows. In that way beauty advisors have of talking about "day into evening" makeup as if insufficient smokiness was your biggest worry in the world.

As she works, Donna translates the hallucinogenic elegance of the Paris runway into the local language. She brushes off overstatement. The swooning exaggerations and glorious loop de loops are now an unspecific, inchoate shimmer around the mom's eyes. At the end of an hour, the two teenagers don't seem to be wearing much more than lip gloss and a little mascara. The mom's eyes are darker and more made up than when she came in, although nothing untoward for chauffeuring the girls back home and getting dinner together.

The bill comes to $135.21 for lipstick, exfoliator, and eye shadow. But that's not all they're getting. Donna races around, scooping up samples. She loads their little bag with lagniappe: brochures, skin care packets, fragrance cards. Everyone gets an application chart that says "From the Runway to Your Way," filled with reminders on "Making the runway look you love yours alone." When she discovers that mom's favorite perfume is a floral fairy tale called Diorissimo, Donna decants a tiny vial as a souvenir. As if any of them were going to forget.

Antsy now, the girls talk about the football game and the dance tonight. The Dior bag dangles from the mother's arm as she signs the receipt. "I came here for something different," she blurts, sounding as though she's justifying herself, "Otherwise I do the same damn thing every day, you know?"

On the counter, the *défilé* plays and the Proustian heroines parade in their endless loop as Dior's new customers happily head for the parking garage with their own versions of the story.

Every so often, some hotshot comes along and decides that makeup might sell better if it was based on something like market research. He—it's almost always a man—rolls his eyes at the idea of a billion-dollar business based on storyboards concocted from magazine pictures. He makes fun of mumbo-jumbo from trend forecasters. He pretends he can't understand what paintings in Paris have to do with eye shadows outside Seattle. Inevitably, he opts for a no-nonsense approach.

Inevitably, disaster ensues. When the Helena Rubinstein brand belonged to Colgate-Palmolive back in the 1970s, one corporate wiseguy decided to install an on-counter computer offering color based on objective analysis. A flop. In the 1990s, a mass-market brand called Clarion tried a gadget it also called a computer. Clarion went out of business soon after. A few years later, Elizabeth Arden came out with computerized custom foundations. Another no-go.

Most recently, E-commerce entrepreneurs bet millions that women would buy perfumes online without being able to smell them, pick lipstick shades without smudging them on the back of their hands, dispense with those sympathetic nods from beauty advisors, and wait patiently for impulse purchases to arrive by mail. Another fiasco. Beauty, which E-entrepreneurs considered a can't-go-wrong commodity, went wrong. Stripped of its stories and reduced to the sum of its parts, makeup didn't seem like much. Even standbys didn't sell well.

Thus far, the only successful "computer" has been Clinique's, which isn't one. To use the abacus-like contraption, a customer slides a few levers around, and thereby discovers whether her skin is oily, sensitive, dry, or combination—in case she doesn't already know— whereupon she still has to turn to the beauty advisor to find out how to get rid of the pimples or wrinkles that brought her there. And, although Chanel has a similar skin-care gimmick (Chanel's spins, Clinique's goes side to side), neither company has tried the idea with color cosmetics.

What a woman wants from makeup can't always be quantified. Market research will tell you that a woman likes lipstick that doesn't melt in her purse on a hot day. A foundation that feels a little lighter. A mascara that sticks to lashes instead of running down cheeks. But facts and figures can't explain what makes her come to the counter. Or come back. They can't explain the customer who craves parole from a life sentence of logic and low prices. Or what an hour pledged to pure vanity represents to a working mom. Stories are better for that.

• • •

"This is never gonna go away," says Debbie Danekas, watching another installment of a long-running love story having its happy denouement. "They *adore* this!" declares Debbie, gesturing to the romantic "Winter Beach" display on the counter behind her. "You'd be amazed at how many women sit in that chair and end up buying the whole thing."

Debbie has her theories about why some color stories sell so well. Instant gratification leads the list. "We make this easy," she says. "If you need a change or you have problems, you might not have the money for new outfits or you might be a couple of pounds overweight . . ." and she finishes that thought with a meaningful nod toward the testers of Ice Storm and Winter Rose and Glacier Berry.

For all the arcane aesthetics trotted out in Dominique's office last year, "Winter Beach" looks easy enough to understand. Its lipsticks and nail polishes are more-or-less pink. Some a little purply. Some a little gray. On the placard, the spokesmodel is snuggled under a big blanket wearing one of those half-smiles that can be read as almost anything. The only thing out of the ordinary is the kicker, a silver-blue gloss called Winter Beach Lip Lacquer—and that was the first to sell out. "Depending on your needs," says Debbie, who uses the word "needs" a lot when she talks about makeup, "you can apply it alone or over something else. It's trendy, but anyone can wear it."

When women come to the counter wanting to know what's new, Debbie can tell them how "Winter Beach" fits in with anything and everything. The store gave her a runway rundown, then the brand gave her another. "We" she says, meaning Lauder, "see the runways and it's so annoying. You say, 'Well, why would we relate to that?' But you scale it down."

Nobody is left out. Nobody leaves a counter unhappy. Women come in clutching pages from *Allure* or *InStyle* and Debbie "works with their needs, so they can be a part of it." If a customer looks awful in the shades being promoted, she takes artistic license. "There's always something in the same spirit that they can wear," she explains, throwing her arms open to embrace all those thousands upon thousands of eye shadows and blushes and lipsticks around her, an alphabet of possibilities with infinite potential for creating stories.

By next week, the first official day of fall, "Winter Beach" will be long gone. Off the counter. Sold out. As it is, the Winter Beach gloss is gone and Debbie's down to her last Sultry Blush (hidden under the register for a customer coming later today). Color stories are set in a near future, a dream time, a season that is always imminent but never arrives. Before the calendar can catch up, they disappear.

Soon she'll have another story to sell. "Holiday!" she says eagerly. "That's gonna hit at the end of October." Debbie's already fired up about its "blazing reds" and "divine whites." New novelty compacts will be here too. Along with sparkly eye shadows and perfumed candles and gift sets. Onward and upward.

. . .

There's always something good going on in the beauty department. There always will be.

In another month or two, Debbie will have lipsticks that look even better—more *au courant*—than the pinks on counter now. Someone will come up with another way to package lipsticks and eye shadows that seems irresistible. Another feisty entrepreneur will start her own makeup line. Next week's New York shows will yield a bumper crop of impossibly lovely faces to be featured in magazines full of beauty ads and beauty editorials. Makeovers and gifts with purchase and promotions will convert new customers and reaffirm the faithful. The holiday color story will be here, and Debbie will be explaining to her customers how it "works with the needs they have."

"You cannot say: 'Okay, next fall it's grayish and purplish lipstick—and that's it,'" Dominique Szabo says, summarily dismissing such directness with a wave of her hand. "You put them in the right mood. You explain why it's so beautiful.

"You tell them a story. Like Aerin was saying: It's like creating a story for children." Dominique doesn't mean to sound condescending. After all, no matter how many of these stories she makes up, she's always the first to fall for them herself.

Like the best storytellers, Dominique relates her air-drawn reveries as if they are absolute truths, broaching no doubt, summoning details to support the illusion, convincing each listener that she herself believes every word. In her version of "Winter Beach," there are no sales projections or sell-through statistics or demographics. Dominique invokes rocks worn smooth by tides, driftwood shaped by weather, and the worlds she sees in a grain of sand. Sounding like a woman who subsists on a diet of fashion magazines with poetry for periodic dessert, she rhapsodizes about art-world arcana and ridiculous refinements like boiled cashmere. She conjures supermodels on runways, masterpieces in Paris, breathtaking luxury, life-changing innovation.

It doesn't matter that her story's audience has never seen a runway show except on television. It doesn't matter that she may be addressing women who have never heard of van Gogh, much less Millet. "Most people don't know," she admits. "So you try to explain. And then they start to dream." They get into the mood of the season. They see shades of meaning in the shades of pink. Makeup becomes more than pigment put in pretty packaging. Makeup is a way to own a beautiful object, acquire the latest technology, wear a fashion right off New York runways, look like Cindy Crawford, live the life promised on the pages of your favorite magazine, espouse feminism.

"There is a lot of romance in the beauty business," Dominique says, looking a little dreamy herself. She glances around the room and her eyes get that wide, slightly glazed expression again, as if she is really seeing windswept, wintry beaches where there are fabric swatches and strange pictures of skinny girls and stacks of old magazines. She starts to add something for emphasis, then pauses, regarding the world from the prosperous perspective of the Lauder offices. Dominique likes the long view.

Finally she repeats, "There's a lot of romance."

ABOUT THE AUTHOR

MARY LISA GAVENAS has been the beauty editor for *Glamour, Mirabella,* and *InStyle* magazines. She has also worked for companies such as Avon, and Yves Rocher, produced magazines for Mary Kay, and covered beauty for publications ranging from *Elle* to *Family Circle*.